LEISURE

Toward a Theory and Policy

Proceedings of the International Seminar on Leisure Policies

Jerusalem
11–14 June 1979

Sponsored by:
Israel Leisure and Recreation Association
European Leisure and Recreation Association
The Hebrew University of Jerusalem, Department of
 Physical Education and Recreation
The City of Jerusalem, Department of Youth, Sports,
 and Social Activities

LEISURE

Toward a Theory and Policy

Edited by Hillel Ruskin

Rutherford ● Madison ● Teaneck
Fairleigh Dickinson University Press
London and Toronto: Associated University Presses

GV
4
.I62
1979

Associated University Presses
440 Forsgate Drive
Cranbury, NJ 08512

Associated University Presses
25 Sicilian Avenue
London WC1A 2QH, England

Associated University Presses
2133 Royal Windsor Drive
Unit 1
Mississauga, Ontario
Canada L5J 1K5

Library of Congress Cataloging in Publication Data

International Seminar on Leisure Policies (1979 :
  Jerusalem)
  Leisure, toward a theory and policy.

  Includes bibliographical references.
  1. Leisure—Congresses.   2. Leisure—Government policy
—Congresses.   I. Ruskin, Hillel.   II. Israel Leisure
and Recreation Association.   III. Title.
GV4.I62   1979   790'.01'35   82-48608
ISBN 0-8386-3134-7

Printed in the United States of America

Contents

Introduction

The importance of leisure has increased in Israel as well as in many other advanced societies throughout the world. The main concern regarding this development is to utilize free time so as to help a person to adapt himself to his civilization and to promote his self-development. The contemporary person is formed not only by his work, but also by the life he leads in his free time. The meaning of leisure for the development of the individual depends upon the manner in which free time is utilized. The ability to exploit free time wisely does not come by itself with increasing free time; people acquire it as a result of appropriate environment, suitable social conditions, and education for leisure.

The task of any government in modern society is to find ways by which the individual can attempt to make use of the possibilities of leisure without succumbing to its hazards. These ways should aim at determining human behavior during free time that will be of recreational and cultural standards acceptable by the society, standards that create a worthwhile style of life. Education brings about great changes in the whole way of life and thus exerts an influence on leisure behavior. However, the best results are possible only when other environmental conditions are available or improved and various parts of the society are motivated to act. These results include a greater awareness and more action by the government in providing opportunities for recreation and the preparation of adults for a wiser and better use of free time; more action on the part of local authorities in maintaining an attractive and healthy environment that provides facilities and opportunities for leisure; and more attention to the role of leisure

7

by the family, public and private organizations, institutions, industry and labor unions, social welfare agencies, commercial recreational enterprises, and the media of mass communication.

In initiating and developing a new approach to leisure, the government is the key institution. Through legislation and public services, the government can spread enlightenment in regard to leisure and the wise use of free time and can make known its attitude toward and concern for the leisure of the people. It can establish a national policy on leisure and formulate the means to achieve this policy. Through programs of public education, the government can promote education for leisure. Through various agencies, the government can develop statewide cultural and recreational facilities and resources and can offer a variety of cultural and recreational opportunities, experiences, and programs. Agencies in local settings, together with public, private, and commercial groups, can enhance these efforts. The whole program for the wise use of free time—involving the schools as well as the communities, industry, and channels of mass communication—can be coordinated in order to bring about maximal results.

All industrialized or Western nations make provision for leisure and regard it as an important issue or governmental function because of the alternatives it provides for healthy, constructive, and socially desirable uses that promote mental health, physical fitness, and other significant positive outcomes. Such alternatives are provided in contrast to passive, antisocial, or self-destructive activities that undermine health, morale, or even economic enterprise.

Leisure in Israel, as in any other modern society, is a central issue. With the technological and socioeconomic developments of the country, with the rise in the standard of living, and with more free time for many people, the emphasis is on leisure, and work is performed more as a means than as an end in itself. Any modern society must be aware of the problems, risks, and challenges posed by free time. The entry of Israel into a civilization of leisure requires special attention on the part of the government to make free time a life-enriching experience. With present-day pressures, free time may be a vital refuge in which the people can find happiness through worthwhile experiences. To this end, the International Seminar on Leisure Policies was organized, and the following recommendations for leisure policies that came as a result of it are offered. It is the hope of the participants of the seminar and members of the Israel Leisure and Recreation Association that these recommendations will trigger the implementation of a leisure policy for the State of Israel.

LEISURE

Toward a Theory and Policy

Part 1

SEMINAR RECOMMENDATIONS

Issues Underlying National Policies for Leisure in Israel

All industrialized nations today provide programs and facilities related to recreation and leisure,[1] through educational institutions, community centers, parks, and other governmental agencies. The following social factors compel a systematic review of national policies supporting the culture of leisure today in the State of Israel:

1. The amount of free time has grown steadily in Israeli society, due to longer vacations, retirement policies, and national holidays. With the present consideration of the five-day workweek, it is essential that leisure programs, facilities, and policies be carefully analyzed for the most effective government functioning in this area of modern life.
2. Within the historical tradition of Judaism, the Sabbath, traditional holidays, and the leisure they offer represent important cultural values. In a world of rapidly shifting moral attitudes, it is essential that these values be reaffirmed and enriched. Other important cultural traditions of the state may also be carried on through leisure programs.
3. Particularly in Israeli society, where wars and continuing threats to national security have created a state of anxiety and tension for many citizens, it is essential that leisure involvements provide relaxation, self-expression, and an improved quality of life for all.
4. In a pluralistic society, marked by different ethnic, racial, and religious groups, it is neccessary to have intelligent policies that will meet the diverse leisure needs of

15

all citizens, enriching their cultural lives and promoting favorable intergroup understanding. Similarly, there is a strong need to provide effective recreation programs to meet the social needs of such special populations as the physically or mentally disabled, the aged, and adolescents. Further, it is suggested and urged that special laws be enacted or agreements be reached with minority groups within the country to insure their rights and the preservation of their unique cultural and recreational patterns and traditions.

5. Although labor shortages and economic pressures in Israel have caused many individuals to work at more than one job, there is evidence of dissatisfaction with work and a growing lack of pride and commitment to work roles. Social scientists agree that leisure can make an important contribution in this area by offering pleasurable and creative alternatives to work in free time, helping workers restore their energies or permitting an extension of work interests, and generally making life more enjoyable and significant.[2]

6. Israel is at present a largely sedentary society with an extremely high rate of television viewing and limited physical activity. Research suggests that this condition may be linked to the nation's high rate of cardiovascular disease. A more vigorous program of lifetime sports and fitness activities during leisure would make a major contribution to the health of all Israelis.

7. As Israel becomes increasingly urbanized, with attendant congestion, pollution, noise, and other stresses caused by high-density living, it becomes essential to provide improved leisure programs and services to improve mental and social health, to relieve tension, and to offer enjoyable outdoor recreation and education opportunities.

8. With the continued growth of industry, agriculture, and residential development, land-use policies must be reexamined to insure the protection of the nation's land and water areas and the preservation of open space for leisure uses, according to ecologically sound principles.

9. Tourism and other forms of commercial recreation have become increasingly important sources of revenue

in the modern world. Leisure opportunities, resources,
and programs need to be carefully planned on all levels
in order to encourage and stimulate this aspect of Israeli
national life.

10. With the possibility of further moves toward peace in
    the Middle East, leisure policies should include prepa-
    ration for, planning of, and participation in joint leisure
    activities with neighboring states, including cultural ex-
    change; sports and art events; visits of teams, delega-
    tions, and citizen groups; book exchanges; and re-
    search, conferences, and scientific exchanges.

11. Finally, it must be understood that leisure has become
    widely recognized by social and behavioral scientists
    and in policy statements of international organizations
    as an important contributor to healthy physical, social,
    emotional, and intellectual development and to the
    overall quality of modern life.

NOTES

1. *Leisure*, in this text, is used primarily as referring to physical, social, intellectual,
aesthetic, and civic experiences in nonwork, or free-time, rather than as referring to a
"state of mind."

2. An important implication of a holistic and humanistic view of leisure is suggested by some participants of the seminar. They suggest a shift away from a concern
with specific types of activities and/or free-time periods and toward a subjective
"state of mind" conception of leisure. Such a viewpoint does not necessitate a splitting
of the person's life into two halves—a work part and a leisure part—but rather deals
with the total conditions relevant to the improvement of the quality of life. Therefore,
it is claimed, an attempt should be made to create conditions that maximize the
generation of the leisure experience throughout the life cycle of the person and in the
total environment of the people; that is, during both free-time and when possible
during job time.

Statement of Policies

Our concern is with the quality of life; central to that concern is a desire to improve the well-being of all the people. A multifaceted approach that includes education, social awareness, and political action is required.

Appropriate political action will be produced by elected legislators who understand the need for and appreciate the contributions of recreation and leisure in improving the quality of life. Legislators who have this understanding and appreciation are best able to develop policies that are based on human needs and also to anticipate the future. Their foresight will increase the likelihood of wise contemporary planning and legislation in terms of reserving land facilities, funds, and other necessary and desirable resources so that future needs will be met.

We recommend that the following ideas be used as a guide in the formulation of leisure policies:

I. The development of a new consciousness of leisure through education should be implemented in the family and school, through informal education, through the mass media, through those who are responsible for conducting leisure activities, through consumer education programs, and through political discussion. The goal should be a reorientation of the attitudes toward and implementation of varied and balanced leisure and recreation patterns of behavior.

II. Equality of opportunity and provision of a core of essential services or opportunities for all should exist and should include such special groups as the disabled, the

18

deprived, the economically disadvantaged, and older adults. These services and opportunities are critical in maintaining the quality of life and community well-being.

A. Within the concept of equality of opportunity, there is the need to consider providing more services and support to the disadvantaged in order to enable them to achieve some degree of equality.

B. Within the concept of equality of opportunity, there is the need to integrate the disabled into all facets of community life.

C. Wherever feasible, commercial recreation should be encouraged so that those who are able to avail themselves of the opportunity do so, thereby easing some of the pressure on scarce government and community resources.

D. There should be an ongoing discussion on the concept of equality of opportunity.

E. The role of government should be to promote and facilitate equality of opportunity for all.

F. Although creative opportunities should be provided for all persons in such areas as arts, crafts, hobbies, and nature studies, provisions should be made for talented persons and groups in the arts, sciences, sports, and other fields.

III. Each level of government—national, regional, municipal, and local—should be encouraged to function in its own appropriate areas.

A. Cooperation, coordination, and consultation among the various levels of government are prerequisite to sound planning and wise development of resources.

B. Leisure and recreation councils should be established at appropriate locations and should function
   1. in an advisory capacity to various levels of government, thus providing grass-roots involvement;
   2. to assist in the organization of the community in leisure and recreation activities;

       3. to disseminate information and publicize leisure
         and recreation programs; and
       4. to preserve, encourage, and enhance pluralism.

IV. It is the responsibility of the government to insure that
everyone has the opportunity for a minimum level of
exposure in the widest range of leisure and recreation
activities.

    A. To insure maximum equality of opportunity on a
continuing basis, everyone should be exposed to the
widest possible range of activities and pursuits.

    B. Provision of facilities should be guaranteed. The
potential of present facilities should be maximized
through multifunctional use. Facilities for the future should be planned with flexibility that would
enable adaptation for varied uses, modes, and life-
styles.

V. Although the government should assume a major role
in implementing leisure and recreation policies, all sectors of society should have a place in the provision of
recreation services. Government alone cannot meet the
pressing and diverse recreational and leisure needs of
the people. Therefore, all interestsed agencies of the
community should be called upon to participate and
assist in the advancement of this endeavor.

VI. A public education and interpretation campaign should
be undertaken to apprise the population of existing
facilities, programs, and opportunities.

    A. This campaign could be conducted both by the
local municipalities and by the national government.

    B. The mass media could be encouraged to become
involved, and this valuable service would enhance
their own functions.

VII. Schools should play a leading role in education toward
the wise use of free time. The public school has children under its jurisdiction during their formative years
and should therefore assume major responsibility in

education for leisure and in initiating leisure preparation for the entire community.

A. In order to achieve the goals of leisure education, the public school should prepare children and youth

1. to judge values and select those which are the highest and most durable;
2. to become aware of the nature and function of leisure;
3. to evaluate and select leisure activities;
4. to determine goals and standards for leisure behavior;
5. to be aware of and understand the scope of the wise use of leisure in society; and
6. to know the basic and advanced skills for leisure activity.

B. This preparation should develop well-rounded men and women who have attitudes, interests, motivations, habits, knowledge, appreciations, and skills that are applicable throughout life for the wise use of leisure.

C. Leisure education should be part of the school curriculum or formal education as well as a part of extracurricular activities or informal education. Through the enhancement of skills, the children should reach states of competence, success, and creativity, thus insuring the personal growth of each pupil.

D. The school should make the learning process in all school subjects an enjoyable experience by innovative practices that affect the learning process and make it exploratory, playlike or recreational.

E. The school should play the role of an agent and "animator" for spreading leisure and recreation practices in the school's neighborhood, involving the pupils, their parents, and other members of the community.

F. The program of leisure education should prepare
    children to reach a high quality of life and to use
    leisure wisely through leisure expressions that have
    the potential to contribute to the intellectual, aes-
    thetic, social, and physical development of the indi-
    vidual as well as through his preparation for resting
    during leisure.

G. The program of leisure education should provide
    experiences that assure personal development of the
    society through
    1. creative expressions that on their highest level
        reach the form of art;
    2. social development expressed by companion-
        ship, belonging, and cooperative group expres-
        sions;
    3. the stimulation of participation in and respect
        for various patterns of leisure behavior of dif-
        ferent cultures;
    4. the enhancement of leisure expressions that
        cause intermingling of patterns of leisure be-
        havior that promotes cultural integration and
        social cohesion;
    5. the provision of skills, attitudes, and apprecia-
        tions necessary for the enjoyment of the out-
        doors;
    6. the provision of physical activity that will con-
        tribute to healthful living through the skillful
        use of the body;
    7. the provision of a wide variety of social, coedu-
        cational, and individual activities that have
        carry-over values for the pupil's future leisure
        as well as those values that satisfy his interest
        during school years;
    8. the assurance of the extension of professional
        leadership and existing facilities to all pupils
        and the avoidance of an emphasis on the excel-
        lence of the few talented ones;

9. the provision of adapted programs for the handicapped;

10. the provision of guidance and counseling programs that lead pupils toward self-direction and self-realization for the wise use of leisure and the attainment of the leisure experience;

11. the provision of activities that encourage participation in voluntary roles; and

12. the cooperation between the public schools and the youth movements.

VIII. Encouragement should be given to the home and the local community as centers for leisure activity. Since more free time is spent at home, within the family circle, consideration must be given to those activities which have a direct influence on the individual's value system.

A. Wherever possible, in the planning of residential complexes, some areas should be reserved for recreation and leisure activities.

B. Within the local community, encouragement and support should be given to leisure and recreational activities and to identification with neighborhood culture and leisure.

C. All school facilities should be available for use by the entire community, as far as is possible.

IX. A multidisciplinary and multiprofessional approach should be utilized. Planning for and implementing a wide array of leisure and recreation activities benefit from the involvement of many disciplines and the gamut of professionals.

A. A campaign of active recruitment should be undertaken to involve a wide range of disciplines in the study of leisure and research.

B. The involvement and advice of a wide range of professionals should be pursued.

C. There should be a continuing program of both scientific research and action research, in collabora-

tion with other disciplines, into the nature and
function of leisure.

D. Professional development and preparation should
   be implemented on a university level.

X. Innovative measures should be explored and exploited.
In view of the limited material, natural, and human
resources available, new approaches, inventive patterns, and innovative procedures should be tried.

XI. Attempts should be made to break down the existing
dichotomy between work and leisure so that both can
be seen as contributing to the quality of life and meeting fundamental needs.

A. Efforts should be made to change work and the
   work environment so that they become psychologically appropriate to most people in the labor force.
   Industrialists, executives, and trade unions alike
   should be aware of the potential benefits of industrial and labor recreation and should be motivated
   to develop it.

B. With the appropriate perception of leisure and its
   significance in modern life and society, workers
   should be encouraged to use their increasing free
   time in meaningful and creative ways, rather than
   with guilt or in passive and superficial ways.

XII. Attempts should be made to maintain close contacts
with other nations and with the international community for the exchange of information, views, and research through conferences and exchanges of faculty
and students.

Part 2

ADDRESSES

Opening Addresses

Gustav Mugglin, Secretary, European Leisure and Recreation Association

On the occasion of the opening of this seminar, it is a great honor for me to welcome you and wish you a very successful meeting on behalf of the European Leisure and Recreation Association. Actually, I am speaking to you in place of a great person who unfortunately is not among us anymore. It is he who would have been the right person to speak to you today. I am thinking of our mutual friend, Norman Lourie. This extraordinary man loved this country and initiated the Israel Leisure and Recreation Association, belonged for many years to the board of directors of the World Leisure and Recreation Association, and was at the same time initiator and foundation member of the European Leisure and Recreation Association. What impressed me most about him was that he as a worldly-wise man recognized the importance of leisure. And he was fully engaged in an improvement of the conditions of living in this matter.

Leisure is much more than the consumption of time. Leisure is a part of time that for millions of people is the only way to realize themselves and to develop their own personalities. This is the reason that leisure has become more and more an urgent social and cultural duty mainly for the industrial countries. Since the foundation of the European Leisure and Recreation Association, we have become engaged in leisure politics of the authorities on a local, regional, and national basis with the aim of getting more humane housing developments

27

and towns, sufficient recreation areas near the cities, and better holiday offers. On the other hand, it is important to find methods and to train animators who are able to show individuals the way to knowledge of themselves, to their own creative imagination, to critical personal judgment, as well as to social responsibility and understanding.

In this regard, we would like to thank the organizers for the realization of this seminar from which we are expecting interesting contributions and ideas for our work in Europe.

Eliezer Shmueli, Director General, Ministry of Education and Culture, the State of Israel

I have the pleasure of opening the meeting. I would like to thank you, first of all, for uprooting me from my office and inviting me to this very quiet, peaceful atmosphere of your international seminar. I usually think of international conference as thousands of people hustling and bustling, and it is nice to sit around a peaceful table and discuss quietly matters that relate to the quality of life.

The truth is that, unfortunately, in Israel there is a tendency to import concepts, as well as different cultures, from abroad. I am afraid that if Israel will not be ready psychologically and technically to absorb the ideas that some of you may raise at this conference, it will fail to implement these very ideas. The very rapid growth of our society, as well as of our educational system and its complexity, present problems in this subject that I assume Israel will have to solve according to its own means of implementation. In Israel we still have two social sectors, one of which has the means and psychological preparation to use its leisure time in a positive way. Unfortunately, there is another sector that, due to its socioeconomic background and its psychological frustrations in the process of absorption into the State of Israel, is not yet ready. Thus I can see today, in the State of Israel, a gap that has broadened during the last years between those who have and those who have not; between those who are using facilities and free time and enjoying life, and others who fail to do so. If that gap continues to grow, we may be facing social disturbances in our own society. Furthermore, one problem that I believe you should bear in mind is the problem of our weekend and our Sabbath.

The religious Jew, in the State of Israel as well as abroad, has his own concept of using his leisure time on his free day, and it so happens that there are misunderstandings as to the way of using the Sabbath between those who do not keep the Sabbath in a traditional way and those who do. I assume that my learned colleagues will deal with these problems to the enrichment of our discussion, and I am sure that we will listen to, absorb, and implement the ideas that will be discussed at this conference where they fit the very special circumstances of our country. One additional thought before I conclude: Israel is one of the few countries in the world that one cannot leave by car. You can leave by flying abroad, but to pick up a car the way Europeans do is impossible here. We are about to grant visas to Israelis who might be using their cars to visit Egypt, our newly friendly neighbor. I assume that you, especially my Israeli friends, should bear in mind that once this claustrophobia is mentioned, the Israeli might be pushed by every motive that he can think of into Egypt. Using leisure time might raise political, psychological, and social problems that we would like to avoid.

I wish you a pleasant discussion and a pleasant stay in the city of Jerusalem, and we could not offer a warmer welcome than we do in this beautiful recreation center.

Yaakov Gil, Director, Department of Youth, Sports, and Social Activities, the City of Jerusalem

I was pleased to receive an invitation to bring you greetings from the city of Jerusalem and from its mayor, Teddy Kollek.

We are holding this seminar in the beautiful recreation center in the forest of Jerusalem. The center serves not only for seminars. We have a saying that all shoemakers walk without shoes. I hope that the participants in this seminar who are working on leisure-time and recreation activities will use the recreational facilities of the Center. . . .

So on behalf of the elected people in the city council and the professionals who are trying to develop leisure-time activities in Jerusalem as a concept and means, I would like to express our hope that this seminar will assist us in developing ideas for leisure policy for Jerusalem as well as for the whole country.

I would like to say a few words about Jerusalem and its leisure needs. It is a unique city within the State of Israel. You will see ethnic groups and the three main monotheistic religions—the Muslims, the Jews, and the Christians—who are trying to develop a harmonious community and a peaceful city and to allow every part to develop itself under its beliefs. We hope that the city of Jerusalem will be assisted in this process. So it was very natural to react to the opportunity to cooperate in organizing this seminar. We must assist any efforts to develop a leisure policy, and the city of Jerusalem is proud to have you here with us.

Problems of Leisure and Culture in a New Nation: The Israeli Experience

Elihu Katz

Let me start by looking at this whole subject from the point of view from which I come to it—namely, from the point of view of mass communications. I became interested in leisure because of my interest in mass communications. A recent study that we did, which was published only a couple of years ago, about five years after our book on leisure,[1] was on broadcasting in the Third World. We looked at the establishment of radio and television broadcasting in the countries of the developing world and had a glimpse from this vantage point of the problems of new nations. And it is quite interesting to see, or to hear, how the introduction of television is proclaimed by the leaders of new nations. They get up and say: Our government has decided to introduce television into our country, despite its very heavy cost, for three reasons: (1) because we have many tribes, language groups, and regional sectors, and we need to integrate them into our society; (2) we wish to use this great new medium for the promotion of social and economic development; and (3) we wish to use it as a means to a renaissance in self-expression, in giving voice to our culture, which has been so long repressed. Six months later, when the station goes on the air, two things will happen. First, broadcasting will be heavily concentrated in the capital city, serving the population that can afford to buy the products that are advertised. Second, the main program in answer to the three aims of integration, socioeconomic development, and cultural

Elihu Katz, Ph.D., is chairman and professor, Communications Institute, the Hebrew University of Jerusalem, Israel.

authenticity is "Kojak." Now, the disparity between these aims—let us take them seriously for a minute, rather than cynically—and the expression that these aims are given in the programming schedule and in the populations that it is so far serving is really extraordinary and deserves some attention. The last of the three goals (which is often stated belatedly)— that of cultural authenticity—is of particular interest to us. Like Professor Kaplan, I was a consultant in Iran and participated quite a lot in the thinking about the development of their system of mass communications. Of all the countries of the Third World, Iran had the most elegant broadcasting system, in terms of its organization, its sophistication, its resources, and the serious thought that was given to planning radio and television broadcasting. Meanwhile, as they say in radio soap operas, something else was going on: there was a second channel operating. This was the channel of Mr. Khoumeini, who was not operating with magnificent transmitters and helicopters, but was sending messages via telephone and via audio cassettes from Paris to the mullahs in their mosques and to the leaders of the bazaars, mobilizing them into a major network to compete with the shah's national Iranian radio and television. The results were extremely enlightening and traumatic, as we all now know, and leave a lot of room for sober second thoughts about the power of mass communications, about how far modernization and the technologies of mass communications can outrun the culture that they are supposedly designed to serve. Which brings me to Israel.

Israel is better off than most new nations in several respects. Unlike many new nations, which have language problems that they have to overcome in order to integrate, in Israel the cultural policy was very calculated and considered. People actually sat down and thought about which language should be the language of the country, and in that sense it is a very interesting laboratory. The decision to revive and revitalize the Hebrew language was perhaps the most brilliant in the history of the movement that led to the establishment of the state. First of all, it gave all of the groups an equal chance—it did not give either a European language or even an oriental language, such as Arabic, an advantage. Rather, it equalized everybody. Most people did not know Hebrew at all, except for a reading knowledge of prayer and study found particularly among the men, who could often read and understand Hebrew; their literacy was high. But nobody knew Hebrew as a spoken language, and the decision to start with this equalizing language was brilliant. Second, the language was not simply Esperanto. Hebrew speakers were given an instant past of two thousand years of culture; so they not only had something equal, they had something in common, and something in depth. They were offered the key to the whole world of learning and creativity associated with the language. Thus Israeli Jews had a shared culture to begin with, much better and much more developed than that in most new nations that are struggling with the problems of identity and culture.

What is authentic is a problem that many new nations have to deal with. Israel does not have to ask that question. Admittedly it has to test—and it is a difficult test—its current creativity in terms of authenticity; but at least one has a pretty good idea of what authenticity is about. One has a good idea of the authentic traditional rhythm of the seasons, of the week, and of individual lives. There are rituals to take care of those transitions; and some of these rituals have indeed become part of the culture of this state, struggling between the heritage of traditions and the now-familiar modes of modernity.

In addition, Israel has the very interesting advantage of having an audience. The whole world is Israel's audience and has watched it very closely from the very beginning; but I am thinking especially of the instant Diaspora, that is to say, the Jewish communities of the world that watch Israel and are so culturally interdependent with Israel. This makes the culture of Israel more self-conscious than that of many other nations. Being onstage is not easy to cope with either; yet having to understand and deal with people who are following the development of Israeli culture from the outside helps to mold a nation inside. This happened with the development of some of the nations in Europe. It was said by Oscar Handlen, for example, that the Italian nation became real only when many

Italians emigrated to the United States and realized that they had something in common, whereas in Italy they knew only that they had come from certain regions and cities, but they had no sense of common nationality. This is not exactly Israel's problem, but the idea of having an outside audience feeding back reactions is an interesting one.

The cultural problem of Israel is the tension between the heritage of authenticity and the new conceptions of culture imported from the West and is best expressed tangibly in an evening's television viewing. For example, from 50 to 60 percent of the programs broadcast are imported from the United States or from England. Now, this is not a big surprise—actually, even in small and rich countries in Europe, this proportion of 50 percent is often characteristic of imported television broadcasting. In some of the Scandinavian countries, for instance, the proportion of imported television material is that high. It gives good expression to the tension between some kind of local creativity and the importation of a culture from abroad. It does not mean that the other half is necessarily authentic, because sometimes the local creativity is simply based on models imported from abroad. You may not import the program but you import the formula from abroad, and this then becomes a problem.

This problem exists in all of the arts. Ninety-five percent of the films are imported from abroad. Foreign plays and books are often presented in Hebrew as translations from other languages. This is a problem on culture in Israel to which I will return.

We made our study in 1970. Our starting point, to quote Professor Kaplan, who was in part quoting us, is that the Jews invented leisure. One can make the assertion—maybe it is dramatic and does not really matter, but in a certain sense it is fair—that the Jews invented leisure with the concept of the Sabbath. But characteristcally, as soon as the idea was invented, it was taken back again as if somebody had said, "This is the Sabbath, and it is a day of rest and leisure and recreation, but we will now tell you exactly how to use this time."

This is the normative idea of leisure that we discuss in the book; that is to say, do *our* thing rather than *your* thing. This is the great tension between authenticity, or the traditional Jewish conception of leisure, on the one hand and the modern Western conception of "do your own thing" on the other. The Western ideal is to find that which will give you, as an individual, maximum individual expression, something in which you will "find" yourself. The Jewish idea is something in which we will find ourselves, or we will continue on our route, so to speak.

The starting point of our book is to look at the role of leisure in the traditional institutions of Judaism. We find that leisure is really quite central when you think about it. The word itself is hardly used, and it is debatable whether there is in fact a word for leisure in the traditional Hebrew language, aside from the concept of rest and expansiveness implicit in the word *lehinafesh*. In any case, if you look at traditional Judaism from the point of view of modern conceptions of leisure, you find that what we would call leisure institutions are quite central in Judaism. I think of the Sabbath, which I have already mentioned; I think of holidays, which mark the seasons and symbolize important events in the history of the people; I think of reading, which today would be called a leisure activity and which was central to Judaism from the very beginning; I think of study, which is not necessarily equated with reading in modern society, but certainly was in traditional Jewish society; and I think of the notion of assembly, which is getting together for prayer, for study, and for other occasions. Our research tries to relate very contemporary assessments of the round of life in Israel within the context of these traditional institutions. That is to say, we ask ourselves in this book, What is the place of these traditional institutions of the Sabbath, holidays, leisure, study, reading, and assembly in modern Israel? How do these leisure institutions fare in this society? In addition, we inquire into the situation with respect to newer leisure activities, whether watching television or going to the cinema or the the theater or to sporting events. We are concerned with the interrelations between the old and the new, the traditional and modern, the authentic and the im-

ported, and so on. I will briefly discuss each of these traditional institutions of leisure and show you how we did our
work.

Take the Sabbath. The question of the Sabbath has been
central to our discussion here. Now, in examining the fate of
the Sabbath in modern Israel we find, one might say, that
there is a mixture of the traditional and the transformed. The
major point to make is that the notion of the Sabbath is very
much more than a "day off" and seems to be continuing as an
institution that has some special cultural characteristics. More
than two-thirds of the people do something symbolic on the
Sabbath, whether they light candles, have a special family
meal that has a festive character, or do something else that has
some association with the Sabbath. Indeed, the rhythm of the
Sabbath is still very much preserved in modern, secular sectors of Israel. Friday afternoon has some of the quality of the
traditional preparation for the Sabbath, even if it only means
cleaning the car, and the day of rest has, as I say, some aspects
of festivity. Whether this Jewish Sabbath will continue to
have any kind of special character beyond that of the Western
Sunday, remains an important question in the cultural planning and policymaking of this society. Just to give you one
more glimpse of hard data, it is interesting to note that in
1970, 60 percent of the population was against the opening of
cinemas on the Sabbath, and that there was no difference—
and this is most striking—between young and old. Even
though it is widely thought that there is a problem with how
young people amuse themselves on the Sabbath, which is
ostensibly ascetic, there is apparent consensus in keeping the
spirit of the day as it is.

The holidays, like the Sabbath, preserve some of their symbolic character. People find meaning in them, but to varying
extents. And our guess is that people find meaning in the
traditional holidays to the extent that they are able to transform these holidays in a secular direction, to find secular
meaning in the holy days. Now this means that people are
uncovering a dimension of the holidays that exists even in the
tradition. Virtually all of the holidays have a seasonal aspect—

they mark time—and to rediscover that is one of the elements in the process of secularizing these holidays. Many of the holidays have an element of ideology implicit in them, such as the idea of freedom implicit in the holiday of Passover. These elements take on increasing salience for the secularizing group in the society, enabling them to participate in the continuity of these traditional holidays, but to infuse them with different meanings, or rather, to give different weights to the several levels of meanings that are already built into these traditional holidays.

The irony of this kind of transformation is evident in the holiday of Yom Kippur. Yom Kippur, of course, is primarily religious rather than seasonal, national, or familial. One cannot go on a picnic; one cannot find a deep national meaning in Yom Kippur; one cannot use it to mark the change of season because the New Year has immediately preceded it. Such holidays are not easily secularized, and because of Yom Kippur's obvious centrality, thought is given by secular intellectuals to such a holiday. Up to 15 or 20 percent of the society will say that they cannot find meaning in Yom Kippur—it is only a day off—and we think that this is because they cannot transform it in a secular direction.

A point about reading. Israel continues to have a high level of literacy and book reading in comparison with other nations, and this is especially interesting because the average level of education in Israel is not all high. It is true, therefore, that people read in amounts beyond those which we find in other countries among people with similar years of education. However, the institution of reading has taken on a completely different character in Israel. Reading in traditional Jewish society was a much more communal thing. People tended to share the same books; indeed, the best example that one can give is that in the tradition—and this is true of certain Christian churches as well—the same portion of the Bible is read throughout the Jewish world on a particular Sabbath. That is to say, it is the experience of shared reading that was characteristic of the traditional institution of the Book. Indeed, the Book, which was read in a shared way and still is in the synagogue, gave a whole common culture to people who could take heroes, language, and metaphors from this shared experience and contributed to the continuous process of cultural creativity in the society. From the earliest days and until now, there has been a continuous accumulation of creative work based on the original text of the Book; the whole history of traditional Jewish creativity can be read in this way. The irony of the secular transformation of this institution—the institution of the Book—is that while the reading level continues to be high, what is being read and how it is being read have been completely transformed. People are reading in an individuated way; people are reading their own books in their own corners; and the notion of shared reading, except for the occasional best-seller and except for the Book, is much more individuated. The shared experience is gone. The irony of this, even further, is to say that what used to be the portion of the week—*parashat hashavua*—is now the television episode of the week—for example, "Kojak"—which comes back each week, and the whole nation with its one television channel, sits looking at the same stimuli, learning language and heroes, and having something to talk about the next day. Ironically, this is very much like the traditional experience of shared reading of the portion of the week in the Book.

I will try to summarize by pointing out a series of problems that seem to us to be worthy of attention is discussing the question of leisure policy in Israel.

First of all, there is the question of the tension between authentic creativity, authentic institutions, and the modernization of those institutions. I gave an example from the secularization of the Sabbath and the secularization of reading; but the question of the tension between authenticity and modernity is, it seems to me, a central problem of this culture.

A second question has to do with the related problem of the tension caused by "doing your thing." That is to say, to what extent can the society hold together, integrate around a norm of doing our thing, the traditional norm of "let's do the same things," rather than "let each individual strive to develop his own individuality, so that he's different from everybody else"? That seems to me a tension that is implicit in this society and is hardly ever discussed explicitly.

The third problem, which seems serious to me and which we have also heard about, is the question of pluralism in ethnic cultures. As you know, there are many ethnic groups in this society, and there are many cultures from which these people have come. There tends to be a homogenization going on within the broad framework of that which is shared as much of the tradition is shared. There seems to me rather less tension in this area than people think there is, because most of the ethnic groups—European and non-European—tend not to be terribly interested in the preservation of their own groups per se (as political entities, for example), although they are interested in the cultural continuity of the particular religious ceremony, food habits, festivals that are unique to their group, and their popular arts. These pluralistic interests are still fighting for survival, and their fate is still not clear.

A more serious problem is the race between ethnicity and education. Given equal education, the consumption of the arts and the consumption of leisure and culture generally in society is the same. That is to say, a person from Yemen or from Morocco, or his children, given eleven years of education, for example, will behave with respect to the arts and the consumption of leisure and culture very much like someone with eleven years of education who comes from Poland, Russia, or Germany. But the proportion of people with eleven years of education or more who come from Yemen or Morocco is relatively low; and the proportion of people with eleven-plus years of education who come from European countries is relatively high. And thus there is a race between ethnicity and education. If education can catch up with the ethnic gap—that is, if the education system can give equal years of training to people from the non-European countries so that they can catch up with the higher number of years of education of those from European countries—things will be all right. But it is very difficult to do this because the gap continues to grow rather than narrow; it is not that some people go down, it is just that some people go up more. Such gaps exist throughout the world, actually, and not just in Israel, and they are increasing.

A further problem that emerged in our study and that is related to this is the problem of development towns. There are many new towns that have been established in Israel where a lot of thought has been given to planning at various levels; but the use of such facilities and the consumption of leisure and culture in these towns is a problem as we found in 1970, because people do not quite feel at home with the cultural milieu in which these developing towns are situated. That is to say, people tell us in our surveys that they are not able to use leisure as they would like because they "do not have the right kind of companions." We do not know quite what they mean by that, because the policy in Israel in recent years has been for relatively homogeneous settlement. But they may be saying, "We do not much care for people like ourselves"— which is a possibility. Or else they are saying, "We do not like those other guys"—because in each such community there is a mixture of people, in spite of the tendency toward ethnic homogeneity.

I will mention two more problems. One is the question of the shorter workweek, which we have also heard about. There is a very serious policy problem in how to design this extra day and how it can be planned for. Indeed, which day should it be? Almost everybody by now is agreed on Friday as the extra day of leisure. It fits in to the religion—Muslims have Friday as a holiday; it fits the shorter work day on Friday, which is already characteristic of Israeli industry and services. Ironically, the only people who are against Friday and would prefer another day are the educated religious group, and that is interesting because they have least to gain from Friday. Given the seriousness with which they prepare for the Sabbath and the inability to make a two-day weekend, given the restrictions on travel, there is a problem here for those educated religious people who would like a two-day weekend and do not see the Friday-Saturday combination as serving them. But apart from the question of which day, the problem of anticipating the challenge arising from an added day of leisure is a matter for serious thought on the level of cultural policy.

Finally, the last point that I wish to make is that here like anywhere else, the problem of leisure, in my opinion, is that of getting people out of their houses. Maybe there will be a decline in television viewing some day, but so far we are very far from a decline, and there is a general home orientation. Whether culture is really well consumed in the home and whether leisure is best pursued in the home are important questions. A lot of us feel that shared culture, assembly, means going out, and if so, the tendency in modern society to stay in rather than to go out, despite the good weather that we have, is a matter for concern. The proportion of people who go out on an average night is not different from what it is in Europe. In any case, as you can see, there is no shortage of problems in Israel for a conference on leisure policy.

NOTE

1. E. Katz and M. Gurevitch, *The Secularization of Leisure: Culture and Communication in Israel* (London, Faber & Faber, 1976).

Leisure: Toward a Theory and Policy for Israel

Max Kaplan

It is appropriate that this conference opens with a tribute to the late Norman Lourie. For many years he lived here and breathed Israel's history, growth, and visions. He carried with him to the end a private dream of creating a project combining the elements of religion, philosophy, and leisure. In his capacity as vice-chairman of the World Leisure and Recreation Association, he worked with me closely, and I had the opportunity to take his measure. Never a scholar, Norman was open to ideas as the WLRA entered a period of major rethinking about its international purposes and programs. Whether we spoke of World War III, Japan, the United States, the European nations, or Israel, he spoke of leisure always with reference to personal enrichment, creativity, and democratic institutions. Norman would have wanted a living memorial such as this conference and its aftermath. And I knew him well enough to know that he would have subscribed to these statements:

1. The study of leisure in Israel is of the highest importance to our understanding of leisure everywhere; for while the nation shares many characteristics with other societies, it exhibits several unique characteristics.
2. Within Israel, public leisure policy will become increasingly important in the next few decades; indeed, the

Max Kaplan, Ph.D., is an author, lecturer, and consultant in the United States.

directions of such policy will serve as one indicator of national meaning and success.

Israel shares with all industrialized nations the recent miracles of instantaneous communications with the world; an interdependence in its economy and politics with events outside its borders; contemporary insights through the physical and social sciences; and the consequences of rapid modernization upon traditions, values, and social institutions.

There are also several elements here that are unique and may have a direct bearing upon leisure as an area of pertinent study and policy:

1. Israel has strong historical roots and is a gathering of 3 million people whose religious, cultural, communal, and family traditions speak directly to meanings of life beyond survival.
2. Since 15 May 1948, Israel has been involved in major wars and ongoing attacks, thus raising issues of leisure as morale, therapy, instrument of personal strength and internal renewal, or as contributor to positive values.
3. Israel's social and cultural heterogeneity is visible everywhere, with residents from over a hundred nations, representing over eighty languages and dialects, raising policy issues of ethnic independence vis á vis national cultural identity and cohesion.

Israel provides itself and the world with a series of remarkable conditions for research: the position of women, the proximity of kibbutz and private life-styles, and above all, the processes of social change in the dramatic interplay of the old and the new.

Now add to this inventory the newest factor, the tangible beginnings of a creative relationship to Egypt and perhaps a new hope for some regional constructive integration. Given the panorama as the cultural setting in which this conference commences, we dare not begin with a modest, safe, simplistic conception of leisure.

If, for example, by *leisure* we mean small, fragmented bits and pieces—a chess game, a television show, a restless car

44   TOWARD A THEORY AND POLICY FOR ISRAEL

trip—then the topic remains internally disjointed and nation-
ally irrelevant. If, on the other hand, leisure is approached
holistically, emanating from and contributing to personal and
collective values, it is immediately enmeshed with the national
world culture; with dreams, images, social disguises, and a
variety of realities; with therapeutic tools for escape and emotional rehabilitation; and with self-discovery or realization.
The gamut, after all, includes such large prototypes as physical, social, aesthetic, intellectual, and civic activity. Barzini of
Italy speaks of national play symbols to cover up national
sadness; Huizinga analyzes play elements in arts, war, and
law; Pieper sees in leisure a basis of civilization; Dumazedier
views leisure as a major indicator and value of the postindustrial society; Piaget, Sorokin, Aristotle, F .S .C. Northrup,
Max Weber, Freud, Marx, and Simmel—they and others have
taken us far beyond the surface of play, or pleasure, or sociability, or the aesthetic, or travel and far into the world of
man's meanings, the human condition, and—at least in my
writings—the relocation of heaven to earth in a kind of Judaic
reordering of the cosmos through leisure.

The fact is that many levels of culture have always inter-
mingled in Jewish history. Visiting Auschwitz, I saw a picture of the symphony orchestra formed by prisoners. In New
York at the turn of the century, as Irving Howe reports in
World of Our Fathers, the theater and other arts thrived amid
the poverty and adaptations to a strange society. In Israel
itself, a rich creative and aesthetic life has flourished throughout its recent decades of turbulence. A new era of comprehensive rapport with your neighbor nation can only underscore
the search for meanings of life as well as of death. But the
difference vis-á-vis the past thirty years is that knowledge and
insights have accumulated during that time, by which mankind everywhere can think and act in the light of new technology, a holistic social science, and a social philosophy that is
enmeshed with the new physics. It is more than an interesting
coincidence that the treaty was signed, and this conference
takes place, in the one-hundredth year since Albert Einstein's
birth. His largest dream, as yet unfulfilled, was of a quantum
theory by which we could perceive the ultimate interrelation-

ships of all the fragments and elements of being. The new physics is a holistic approach to the world, so that the yin and yang, the animals and plants, the chemical and the geological, the social and the physical, and the processes of birth and death are found within the other, one needing the other, and both essential to the whole. Various expressions of the groping toward an integrated conception are found in such constructions as the oriental and occidental, socialistic and capitalistic, or the functionalist anthropology of Malinowski and the structural-functional approach of Talcott Parsons.

Similarly, the study of leisure can be understood only in the comprehensive framework of the total society. That is, indeed, the first significant implication of this conference: that leisure and recreation in Israel are central, not peripheral, issues.

However, the integrality of leisure and recreation to national cultural theory and policy requires a formidable, comprehensive, and holistic working model to set out a series of potential relationships. I need hardly note here that there is little consensus on the international scene on a formalized conception of leisure; nor, given the nature of social science, does there have to be. Each of us constructs his own tools, sometimes forgetting that they are tools, not gems of truth. in 1971 our Leisure Studies Program, then in Tampa, called a special conference of experts from many nations, including the socialist, devoting three full days entirely to the concept. Of course, afterward each of us went his own way. But there is more need for some consensus here; the outsider has the feeling that both local and national officials in Israel are listening. Your educational leaders have gone through major reorganization. They, at least will ask, What is a reasonable characterization of leisure so that we may proceed on more than an ad hoc level?

With a few notable exceptions, such as my colleague Joffre Dumazedier in France, the Czech scholar Zuzanik (now in Canada), Kenneth Roberts in England, Phillip Bosserman in the United States, and Herald Swedner in Sweden, leisure scholars have not had much to contribute to creative thinking on the cultural level. The reverse has been more to the point:

studies of such cultural-policy institutions as UNESCO and the Council of Europe have themselves turned to the leisure concept. This direction among cultural policymakers was inevitable as, in recent years, these international bodies realized that culture was more than the right of the elites.

The conception I have reached is a Weberian construct of elements. I find that all attempts to distinguish neat packages that are called *work, religion, science, family, education*, and so forth, only feed the myths or unrealities that constitute some contemporary social science. None of these institutions exists within clear-cut boundaries; each consists of very general elements that often overlap. *Work* may have social aspects; *religion* and the *state* are enriched with symbols. The daily realities of living do not go on in neat categories just because that is the way in sociological studies in university catalogs. My mentor and colleague in Illinois, Florian Znaniecki, used the term *human coefficient* to emphasize the need for scientists to see through the eyes of those whom they are studying, rather than through their a priori categories of human action and meaning.

Thus, I view leisure as a relatively self-determined activity experience that falls into one's economically free-time roles; that is seen as leisure by participants; that is psychologically pleasant in anticipation and recollection; that potentially covers the whole range of commitment and intensity; that contains characteristic norms and constraints; and that provides opportunities for recreation, personal growth, and service to others.[1]

The next question in theory is to relate our characterization to a larger set of elements in the society. The strategy in creating the model was to construct four subsystems that could be equally useful in providing a context of relationships for religion, science, education, or anything else. Thus, by putting *leisure* into the center position, we automatically elevate that subject to an institutional level, open to the same strict analytic standards. As a string quartet player, I am comfortable with the fourfold construction. Its purpose, of course, is fully realized only through the interplay of the instrumental

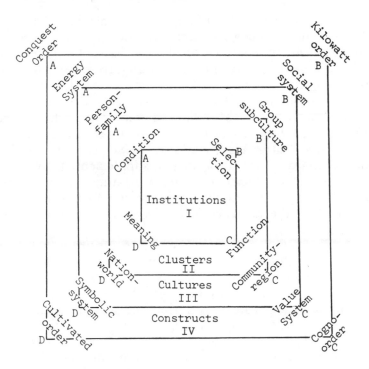

CONCEPTUALIZATION OF LEISURE IN SOCIETY

elements; my 1975 volume should be judged on that basis.[2]
Here I propose a far simpler plan—to extract one issue from
each subsystem with special applications to Israel.

1

The first subsystem suggests that to develop either analysis
or policy, we begin with concrete, objective, measurable items
such as age, income, education, residental location, health,
and discretionary time. My last volume, issued a few months
ago, dealt entirely with the age factor. Permit here some comments on time structure, for the Katz-Gurevitch volume, un-
doubtedly familiar to everyone here, notes the trend toward
adoption of the five-day workweek, and some debate has been

going on as to which should be the additional day of rest. It is
clear that here, as in all Western societies, time has become a
value in itself, an aspiration of all social classes for understandable purposes of personal use, relaxation from work routines,
extended trips, and so on—and not, as Veblen observed,
merely as emulation of upper classes. In the United States
there is now considerable talk of the four-day workweek, and
Poland in 1974 moved in that direction by doubling the number of "free" Saturdays from six to twelve per year. But these
ideas are now replaced, or at least supplemented, by the in-
triguing and sensible concept of a work-time structure based
on individual tests and life-styles, moderated of course by
exigencies of the particular job or its interpenetration into the
work of others.

One third of all workers in West Germany are now on "flex-
time". The OECD in Paris several years ago devoted a full
conference to new work-time structures. The idea has recently been seized upon in the United States, especially by the
California state senate, as offering one way of finding part-
time jobs for the unemployed, because the research finds that
many workers are willing to reduce their own work hours
with the consequent surrender of some income. The new
trade-off stems from the simultaneous decline in the real value
of the dollar, mark or pound and the rising value of the hour
with the growth of alternatives for its use and better material
facilities to implement the selection, as in transportation.

Supporting evidence on the potential of flex-time and flexible arrangements of working years is provided in the United
States by our National Commission for Manpower Policy,
especially in the researches of Fred Best. The familiar "linear"
work life has, indeed, reduced our workweek from sixty hours
to less than forty hours in the course of this century, and the
work hours have been largely compressed into the middle
portion of the lifespan. In a national survey in 1978, Best
found that 45 percent of workers were willing to reduce their
work to part-time, with a corresponding loss of income.[3]

Obviously, the feasibility of flex-time depends on the type

and structure of the job. Bernhard Teriet of West Germany holds that flex-time is "practical and applicable for up to 50–60 percent of all employees."[4]

It may be that Israel offers a unique set of circumstances for such experiments. Here the Sabbath observance by almost all . provides an anchor in the weekly rhythm without the need for an arbitrary selection of a second free day. Further, your growing problem of more elderly persons, as among us, can be approached in part by reducing work time a few years before retirement. Not only can governmental services and offices adjust to flex-time with their own flexibilities, leisure services could do so as well. The gasoline shortage in the United States now introduces another motivation toward flexible work schedules and fewer working days.

The outsider may, therefore, hope that Israel will move beyond traditional thinking about time, especially when individualism and creative thinking are so characteristic of Jewish community life. If, as Heschel holds, Judaism itself is an innovation in the "architecture of time"—with its introduction of the Sabbath—then Israel's work, and therefore its nonwork, structure could serve as a model of social engineering with the flexible-time resource as a major input. Computer techniques have made such flexible time use more feasible to manpower and inventory controls.

For the recreation profession, flexibility then becomes both a response and a stimulus for breaking traditional benefits for what is called the delivery of recreational services. Diana Dunn notes that in the United States, not one city of over half a million provides public recreation in its facilities from midnight to 8 A.M.[5] Yet in Bucharest I have seen a public library, well stocked with books in half a dozen languages, open all night in a public park.

Obviously, flexibility in space goes with time. In the United States presently, from a combination of inflation, a Watergate legacy of suspicion of all government, and the "Proposition 13" mentality that now dominates all political concerns, new interest is being shown in the private or commercial sector as the coming job market for recreation graduate students (more than 37,000 in our country). Israel, in this regard, could become a laboratory for other nations if its policy permitted these flexibilities between work and leisure time.

2

From the second subsystem there are again a multitude of relevant issues. Permit a few comments on II-B, "subcultures," for the ethnic issue is central to Israeli cultural and educational policy.

As far back as 1953, *avodah kehilatit*, or community work, was established as a program to overcome dependency among the immigrants in twenty-one new towns; by 1968 the program had fifty staff persons in thirty-five localities under the sponsorship of *saad*, the Ministry of Social Welfare, and *Amidar*, the national housing corporation. Among the several goals, one has been "to bring different ethnic and religious groups together to improve their social relationships and to develop citizen participation."[6] The result, apparently, is a mixed picture. Katz and Gurevitch conclude from their studies of leisure that "the extent of normative integration in the society . . . is very striking."[7] Yet they report that all groups, whatever their ages or education, wish to maintain a national policy of cultural pluralism. Serious differences still exist among class and ethnic groups. Among the few world scholars who have related leisure seriously to cultural policy, Joffre Dumazedier suggests that the purpose of cultural planning is "merely to apply more rationally to cultural development as a function of each individual's, each group's, each class's and each society's needs."[8]

Repeatedly, the administrators of Israel raise the question, How is a balance to be sought between national identity and ethnic variety? There are many levels of this so-called balance. In respect to proportions of population, less than 15 percent of Israel's population was of Eastern, or non-Ashkenazic origin, subdivided into what Professor Avineri of the Hebrew University calls the Sephardic patriciate, the Sephardic masses, and the Yemenites; by 1973, the proportion of Sephardic and other Orientals had gone to 60 percent. The Orientals have grown in political talent and power, especially in the smaller communities. The issues here are the cultural patterns among the subgroups, or more precisely, whether the European educational, recreational, and aesthetic traditions will continue to dominate in spite of new population proportions. There are forces underlying all of this, including the growing economic equality among these subcultures. The purpose of policy is to promote both the traditional and the innovative elements of the new relationships. In the past year we have seen the price paid when innovation was too rapid for part of the society. This was one of the factors in the fall of the shah in Iran. As a consultant to his Ministry of Culture, I met with his social planners in their attempts to preserve Islamic arts. His recent five-year plans, unsuccessful as they turned out to be, were very explicit in their search for a blend of the old and the new. Currently, in Israel, a strategy of great subtlety and potential impact is taking place in the field of music education. It stems from the method for teaching music to children through their own folksongs and reaching forward into the most contemporary of sounds and understanding. Unable themselves to go to Hungary until now, music educators at Tel Aviv University called upon my wife, Barbara Kaplan, and her long residency in Hungary to introduce the system developed there by Zoltán Kodály. Here, then, is a simultaneous reliance upon innovation and tradition.

The field of leisure, if interpreted to cover the whole range of self-chosen activity, provides an unending laboratory for preserving and innovating—in the arts, education on all levels, the content of television, and so on. Innovations addressed to everyone can remain on the level of distribution of the mass media or can extend to the opportunities given to the blind, deaf, elderly, and to villages of the country; but the policy can simultaneously respect the dignity of traditions found among the subcultures. One would hope that recreation leaders and cultural policymakers here are drawn from a broad base of the population. The Council of Europe has in recent years produced conferences and reports on this point. The contrast they make is between the "democratization of culture" and "cultural democracy." The first phrase is an implicit evaluation of elite culture that should be spread among the disadvantaged"; the second was still stimulated in the anthropological literature by Oscar Lewis and calls attention to what he termed the "culture of poverty," or the dignity of life among even the materially disadvantaged. No one would argue that minorities are culturally deprived, yet in American society this was for a long time the educational attitude toward the blacks and remains our policy toward our Indian children.

The purpose of leisure amid these many ethnic groups must not be to erase differences but to feed them and thereby bring the differences in life-style to a state of consciousness. Leadership in the recreational realm, therefore, performs the function of channeling pluralism away from the conflict areas of politics and toward the areas of play. In politics, conflicts are disruptive; in play, they serve creative purposes.

3

Permit me to offer a brief discussion of leisure as a "social system," a component of the third subsystem on the model. Chapter 13 of my 1975 volume treats various prototypes of leisure as social systems, familiar originally in the work of Joffre Dumazedier as the physical, social, intellectual, aesthetic, and civic. As social systems, each of these types has its respective roles, symbols, spaces, attitudes, times, skills, functions, and restraints. It is a far different approach to activities than a mere tabulation of numbers of people who participate and their expenditures, or even of correlations with education or income. This nation is fortunate to have had, since 1976, the studies by one of our conferees, Professor Elihu Katz of the Hebrew University, and his colleague in England, Professor Michael Gurevitch; both are sociologists. The title of their volume already reveals their central conclusion—*The Secularization of Leisure: Culture and Communication in*

Israel. The data is plentiful. In the rhythms of work and leisure, Israel is like other industrial societies. Sociability and
time for reading and for child care rank high. Most meaningful
of the major holidays is Israel's Independence Day. Yom Kippur, traditionally the most sacred of days, is now "meaning-
less" to sixteen of every twenty Israelis—surely, a contributing item toward the theme of secularization. Among fifty-five
communities sampled by the interviewers, the kibbutzim contain the richest variety and quality of leisure resources; new
settlements have the least. Trips to theaters, museums, and
public parks are frequent. Educational background is most
influential in the choice of daytime activities; age in the choice
of nighttime activities. As throughout Europe, visits to a cof-
feehouse and walking remain important in Israel. Visiting
with friends continues as a frequent activity, with one's education as the main influence on content of conversation. About
half of all free time goes to television viewing. Television
programs are now broadcast on Friday night as well as Saturday, after what must have been a lively controversy; expect-
edly, news programs are most popular, followed by light entertainment. Finally, as the outsider would expect for a
population placing a high value on the mind and the book,
reading and study are esteemed for their own value and as "an
important connection to Jewish tradition." Beyond these em-
pirical findings, Katz and Gurevitch go further than many
students of the field in relating and interpreting their observations to large issues of culture and national policy. We anticipate eagerly the next volume in which they promise to make
these policy implications more explicit.

Religious patterns and education are major variables in
time-use differences. The Sabbath—both Friday evening and
Saturday—is given over to much family visiting, trips, and
rest. Television viewing is largely a family affair. The ethic of
work remains strong. As in the United States, the better
educated are more content with their work and play and
would like more free time.

Among the issues these authors raise is the place of these
patterns in the "attributes of the Jewish people." Their book

title derives from the finding that ethnic attributes far exceed those of a religious nature. "What's more, the young people are as likely as their elders to emphasize the importance of the ethical and the ethnic, and are *less* likely than their elders to agree that religious beliefs and practices are characteristic."[9]

The purpose of this portion of my statement is to suggest the need for a theoretical analysis of activity prototypes in relation to social symbols, needs, and the uniqueness of both national and subcultural patterns. This serves the purpose of leisure counseling and education, and it clarifies the needs of persons who are being served. Programming takes on the dimension of conscious purpose. The preparation of recreation leaders, therefore, calls upon social-psychological awareness of activities as well as of people. Among the special studies reported in the Katz-Gurevitch volume, the place of mass media is especially important. In your country as well as mine, movies, radio, newspapers, and television represent important use of time, both in quantity and impact. But the questions asked by these scholars—both expert in the field of communications—go beyond a simple counting of the public to ask, What do people do with the media? Contrary to Marshall McLuhan, their functional technique of research "argues that people bind the media to their needs more readily than the media overpowers them." They begin with an attempt to identify the felt needs of the population and of subgroups, then the extent to which the media fill those needs. There is no time or necessity here to examine their results in detail. Perhaps the most significant for the conference is the fivefold grouping of sociopsychological needs among the Israelis (Arab residents were excluded from the survey):

1. Needs related to strengthening information, knowledge, and understanding . . .
2. Needs related to strengthening aesthetic, pleasurable, and emotional experience . . .
3. Needs related to strengthening credibility, confidence, stability, status . . .

4. Needs related to strengthening contact with family, friends, and the world . . .
5. Needs related to escape or tension-release . . .

Comfort for the recreation profession can derive from their first conclusion, that "for all needs examined, the non-media sources (combined) were deemed more gratifying than the mass media. Friends, holidays, lectures and work were often said to be more important sources of gratification than the media." For example, "friends are more important than the mass media in needs having to do with self-gratification, even 'to be entertained.'"

Some comments on our current situation in the United States may be of interest. Until recently, inflation was the new focus of our leisure research. The issue was pertinent everywhere in terms of changing life-styles, but especially to the South and states like Florida. The index of tourism became a crucial indicator. To the surprise of many newspaper columnists and politicians, tourism kept expanding. Disneyland in Florida had exceeded attendance expectations by several million in the 1960s (its first years), and May 1979 saw a 13 percent increase over May 1978—this in the face of both inflation and our newest fear, the real or manipulated shortage of gasoline. The near panic over oil shortages did, however, result in deserted highways in many states, especially California, over our recent Memorial Day weekend. If, in fact, the fear continues, or a real shortage is confirmed, far-reaching changes in American life may be expected: shorter trips for pleasure and vacation, more use of community and neighborhood facilities, and more home-centered activity. On the last of these, television's impact will be interesting to observe, for a recent national survey for the *Washington Post* indicated a decreasing use of television, largely because of growing disgust with commercials and the quality of programs. The revolution going on in electronic communications is the key to the future of much leisure in the United States. For example, if pay-TV grows in popularity and, within this, freedom—at a

price—to eliminate commercials and select a higher level of
offerings, one result may be direct broadcasts of concerts, as
from Lincoln Center, and an enormous economic boom for
the arts. Already, federal subsidies to the arts have gone from
$7 million to over $200 million since 1965; as a nation we
already spend annually about $8 billion more for attendance at
professional arts than for all sports. Our total national expenditure for recreation in recent years exceeds the cost of
national defense. There are other significant leisure trends in
the United States, but that is not our fundamental issue here.
I have mentioned some of our issues in the hope that when
Professor Katz and his colleagues relate their findings here to
broad cultural issues, they will treat Israel as a case study
among other technological societies as well as for its
uniquenesses.

It would appear that in both societies the race between
education and technology envisioned by H. G. Wells is not
yet a black-and-white issue; nor, as Jacques Ellul fears, a clear
victory for technological values. Even in Israel, we are told,
women are knitting; men are engaging in sports, games, and
collecting; and many more of both sexes than we supposed are
involved with the arts.

The Israeli school system has understandably focused on
the issue of "integration" since your State Education Act of
1953 and the reforms following the Prawer committees in the
mid-1960s. Those attempts at reform, successful or not,
sought to restructure the schools in order to do something
about the existing social and economic stratification among the
people.

Perhaps, with the rethinking in your new political and cultural situation, the time has come for another look at your
schools in reference to substantive issues on quality of life.
This is a more difficult issue than structural reform for a
pluralistic and democratic goal.

This conference and profession might consider its role in
the introduction of a new educational initiative. The United
States has a similar need to consider a widening of its purposes
and to enlarge the current demand for a return to the "basics."

By that is usually meant the skills of reading, writing, and arithmetic as tools for making a living. The need now is to convince our policymakers that skills in the nature of leisure commitments are equally basic. Educators, however, will react only if the point is made by the society as a whole.

In all industrial societies, then, the need for educational institutions to prepare for leisure and ultimately retirement is well founded. One of my classes was visibly moved a few weeks ago as we discussed life-styles in the postindustrial society. In the United States a twenty-year-old can—by present time use—anticipate a minimum of 35 hours of "free time" every week; even without vacations and the anticipated reduction of work hours per year, this comes to 1,750 free hours per year, and 87,500 over fifty years. That is, by the age of seventy, our current college sophomore will have had an equivalent of almost thirty *years* of free time at the rate of eight hours per day! That is the reason that the LEAP program (Leisure Education Advancement Project) was developed in Indianapolis several years ago, limited to the public schools and funded by a private foundation.

4

We come to the last subsystem of the model, and here I prefer to end with some general comments touching all four components. It is clear that to an unusual, even dramatic, degree, Israel is a "social order" that contains the first three, and perhaps also the fourth, components. Among its residents are some who live as their forebears did centuries ago. They differ from examples in other societies in that they comprise a part of a modern environment, but the force of tradition or religion is as strong as among Arabs, Orientals, or Gypsies.

The second, so-called Kilowatt, type of social order is shared here with industrial societies in Western Europe and parts of the Communist bloc and Japan: technological processes, middle classes, high literacy, rapid change, and so on.

The Cogno social order is transitional, seeking to understand its roots as well as its goals and direction. The Cultivated order, finally, differs from Daniel Bell's more familiar "postindustrial" by paving the way for a blending of moralistic utopias with scenarios that are grounded in realities and trends.

Thus, the model is not devised as a historical order, and that is why I avoid the sequential categories—preindustrial, industrial, and postindustrial. Bell and others have attempted to establish criteria for the last category, with data from the United States, Japan, and Sweden.

The assumption to guide policies for Israel's future is that the country will continue to be in a state of flux, change, and self-evaluation, typifying the so-called Cogno social order. For a long time to come, no matter what its external political or military circumstances, social and cultural stability are unrealistic scenarios. Elements from the past will always remain dominant and mixed in a unique way with Western science, technology, and thought. Both educational and leisure policy, to be realistic, must prepare for and reflect this permanent dynamic.

The first principle for leisure policy is both flexibility in program and depth of content. Event more than in the relatively stable situations of Europe and the United States, people here become the focus rather than formulas for organization or programs. The training of recreation and community workers in such a changing context must be humanistic as well as technical, grounded in philosophy and history, conscious of community structure and social heterogeneity. For example, the evaluation of the recreation program is mistaken if, in the words of a recent letter to me from the Ontario Recreation Society, it seeks to find indexes to measure the so-called soft assessments where they are—on the internal, private, and indefinable level. I am not antiscience; I am concerned that science recognize its limitations. That aspect of recreation and leisure had best be treated through such instruments of language and emotion familiar in aesthetic or humanistic and poetic discourse. This approach requires leaders who are secure individuals, working for flexible but secure administrators.

A second derivative principle with a Cogno social order is

that the leisure-recreation profession is highly interdependent with other agencies and institutions of the community or nation, and even close to international bodies. On the world level, the curriculum for leisure and recreation students should make use of the series of UNESCO cultural policy reports from more than twenty countries and the 1978 reports from the Council of Europe on sociocultural animation. Within the communities to which they are sent for field experiences, young leaders should know the full cultural resources—libraries, theaters, ethnic activities, and so on. If, as is often the case, the national or local government bodies are overly decompartmentalized, the leisure-recreational proponents are in a favorable position to cross lines; their impact upon the schools can help provide a cultural focus. Still in its humanistic role, this profession is also interested in the work context and its improvement. But overall, we may accept for leisure-recreation the concept of responsibilities defined by a 1973 report of the European Foundation for Cultural Development:

> Animation may be defined as that stimulus to the mental, physical and emotional life of people in an area which moves them to undertake a range of experiences through which they find a greater degree of self-realization, self-expression and awareness of belonging to a community over the development of which they can exercise an influence.

Returning, finally, to this association, several directives seem desirable:

1. That this association explore the possibilities of a permanent alliance, perhaps in the form of a joint committee with your ministries of culture and education, based on a resolution from these proceedings. Its purpose would be a comprehensive exploration of common issues and strategies. The mood vis-à-vis the United States may now be ripe for interchange with American authorities and agencies and through your affiliation with the ELRA and its worldwide umbrella, the WLRA, for permanent interchange with educators and recreationists of other nations.

2. That this association explore a permanent relationship with relevant groups and training institutions in Egypt. Following the thinking of the Israeli business community, it is important to pursue a policy of joint action. A statement from Uzia Galil, president of an electronics firm in Haifa, is worthy of note. "It's most important that the first things we do must be successful. The image of success is vital. . . . It's also terribly important that we create a spirit of partnership. We should try to look for Egyptian areas of strength. The worst thing we can do is to try to appear as teachers."

3. That this association join with other agencies of Israel to design the future. My view is that a major result of "futurology" is that the criterion of its success is in large part a different attitude toward the present. The major challenge in all industrial societies is to rethink and restructure their attitudes toward work and nonwork. In my last book, published in April 1979, I raised some questions about the actuality of a work ethic. Did it ever exist? Or rather, did this ethic serve as a convenient myth for the industrial age? For if work, per se, is a fundamental motivation, why does it need a theological rationale? Why is a heavenly reward necessary? And indeed, a reading of English history in the early decades of the Industrial Revolution indicates that villagers and farmers did not flow to Manchester, London, or Liverpool to reach heaven sooner; nor did they hurry to the factories in response to a work instinct. They went to make money. Even with this earthly reward, some had to be recruited by force and with false promises.

There is a more serious objection to the view that the work ethic is our primary value or drive. It is after all, a means; heaven represents the end. Can work be both means and end? This fallacy has been repeated endlessly, yet the paradox exists. Further, what is heaven? A forty-hour week, or any number of hours? The fuzzy concept of heaven, accepted with little elaboration, is that in heaven there is no work and the chosen are forever free to gambol, converse, or, in Sebastian de Grazia's articulation of the Greek view of *paideía* to be led to "beauty, to the wonder of man and nature, to its contemplation and its recreation, in word and song, to be serenely objective." Let us submit a more realistic hypothesis, more in line with the evidence all around us: *The primary value of mankind in industrial societies is leisure.* This is what work permits and frees us to do. In preindustrial societies there is a difference, for then one's work is holistic: the whole farm is cultivated, whole shoes and whole dresses are made. The preindustrial worker does not find himself in an assembly line, with fragmented responsibility and only a fragmented car fender to guide through a machine process under technology's "Saint" Taylor.[10]

Two cautions may be pertinent. One is from our French colleague, Dumazedier, in his 1974 volume: "Those who support cultural planning do not intend to turn rationality in general, and service in particular, into a preferred context for cultural development . . . . and official culture by those in power. It is merely to apply more rationality to cultural development as a function of each individual's, each group's, each class's and each society's needs."[11]

A second warning comes from your renowned authority in policy planning, Professor Yehzekel Dror of the Hebrew University, in his characterization of the social sciences. Among them he notes: "*(a)* oscillation between idiographic microstudies and 'grand theory'; *(b)* a priori commitment to equilibrium and structural-functional concepts, which result in do-nothing, or at best, incremental-change recommendations; *(c)* timidness in falling into social issues and in handling taboo subjects; *(d)* perfectionism which causes withdrawal from problems with time-constraints, that is, all significant policy issues; *(e)* deep feelings of guilt about getting involved in applications which go beyond 'value-free,' 'pure,' 'factual' and 'behavioral' research."[12]

These several directives for goals have only begun to lay some base for more specific considerations of leisure in educational, communal, and labor frameworks. This conference, therefore, is not grafted onto your national life, with leisure only a minor consideration in a larger struggle for economic growth, internal political stability, and peace. The conference can make explicit a philosophical and policy tool of high importance—no less than a framework for unity, comprehen-

siveness, balance, interrelatedness, and the eternal flow from
the "I" to the "thou," from the one to the many, from rational-
ism to existentialism.

A few days ago, I was interviewed in Tel Aviv by a young
journalist writing for one of the Tel Aviv evening newspapers.
We spoke broadly of many issues. She is disturbed about the
antiwork attitudes here and the difficulty of obtaining sustained dedicated work. My response could hardly be on a
factual level. As an outsider, I told her that the material goods
are apparently going forward—buildings, highways, and new
communities. But to me that surprising achievement is not the
material foundation of society, or even indicative of its ability
to survive. These are means and testify to efficiency, good
intelligence, and the will to live and as everywhere are only
the means. But the ends are exemplified or symbolized by the
superb chamber orchestra I listened to in rehearsal at
Shefayyim, made up of thirty fine musicians from kibbutzim
around the country, playing Mozart, Handel, and a contemporary Israeli work; or the dance festival at Dahlia; or the fine
pictures, sculptures, and jewelry we saw in the art galleries of
Tel Aviv and Ein Harod. It is this threefold synthesis or
juxtaposition of creative life, the struggle for survival, and
natural national growth that is the real miracle. This synthesis
needs constant articulation, research, celebration, and nurtur-
ing. This, I suggest, is perhaps your contribution.

NOTES

1. Max Kaplan, *Leisure: Theory and Policy* (New York; John Wiley & Sons, 1975),
p. 26.

2. Ibid. chapter 2.

3. Fred Best, "The Future of Retirement and Lifetime Distribution of Work",
(based on testimony before the Subcommittee on Human Services, Select Committee
on Aging, U.S. House of Representatives, 3 May 1978), p. 2.

4. Bernhard Teriet "The Flexible Time: An Object for the Future," *RPCCNTRES
Europeenness* Du Care de Vie, Paris, Dec. 6.

5. Diana R. Dunn, "Urban recreation," in T. Todbet, *Recreation, Park and Leisure
Services: Foundations, Organization, Administration* (Philadelphia: W. B. Saunders Co.,
1978), p. 47.

6. Ralph M. Kramer, "Urban Community Development in *Israel: Social Structure and Change*, edited by M. Curtis and M. Chertoff New Brunswick, N.J.: M. Curtis, ed., 1973.

7. Elihu Katz and Michael Gurevitch, *The Socialization of Leisure; Culture and Communication in Israel* (London: Faber & Faber, 1976), p. 162.

8. Joffre Dumazedier, *Sociology of Leisure* (New York: Elsevier, 1974), p. 161.

9. Katz and Gurevitch, *Socialization of leisure*, p. 254.

10. Max Kaplan, *Leisure: Lifestyle and Lifespan—Perspectives for Geronotology* (Philadelphia: W. B. Saunders Co., 1979), pp. 16–17.

11. Dumazedier, *Sociology of Leisure*, p. 161.

12. Yehezkel Dror, *Design for Policy Sciences* (New York: Elsevier, 1971), p. 9.

Formal and Informal Education for Leisure-centered Living: Implications for Educational Frameworks

Hillel Ruskin

Introduction

The purpose of this presentation is to suggest principles that may guide public educational frameworks, in modern societies in general and in the State of Israel in particular, in developing curricula for formal and informal leisure education.

The procedures for accomplishing this purpose involve: (1) a study of universal concepts of leisure that may serve as a basis for principles for leisure education; (2) the identification of social, technological, and physical characteristics of society that affect the use of leisure in a particular country; (3) the identification of characteristics of leisure behavior in a particular country; (4) the identification of characteristics of public education that have implications for leisure; and (5) the formulation of principles that should serve to guide public education in developing curricula for education for leisure.

The presentation includes a summary of the study, which resulted in the formulation of thirty-seven principles that may guide any modern society in the education of its citizens for the wise use of leisure. These principles also suggest goals and objectives for leisure education, criteria for the selection of

Hillel Ruskin, Ph.D., is chairman, Department of Physical Education and Recreation, the Hebrew University of Jerusalem, Israel, and chairman, Israel Leisure and Recreation Association.

content of activities and educational channels, and offer desirable characteristics and methods for leisure education.

In initiating and developing an appropriate approach to leisure, the government is the key institution. Through legislation and public services, the government can spread enlightenment with regard to leisure and the wise use of it and can make known its attitude toward and concern for the leisure of the people. It can, and should, establish a national policy on leisure and formulate the means to achieve this policy. Through programs of public education and adult education, the government can develop action toward leisure education. Without the skills and knowledge of leisure education in the school, or without the resources and opportunities provided after school, the wise use of leisure cannot be accomplished. The government should widen the accessibility of leisure education to children and should increase participation of individuals in different forms of recreational and cultural life of the society.

Leisure in Israel is a central issue. With the technological, social, and economical developments of the country, with the rise in individual income, and with more free time for many people, their basic outlook is leisure, and work is performed more as a means than as an end in itself. Israel must be aware of the general problem of leisure. Leisure stands forth as a challenge to Israel, and its cultural level depends on the wise use of leisure. Although many people in Israel are divorced from these wise uses of leisure, the main educational efforts deal with the needs of work and not with the preparation of children for a balanced life of work and leisure. The entry of Israel into a civilization of leisure requires much more attention on the part of the government to making leisure an enriching experience that will lead to a good life for the people.

Suggested Principles for Educational Frameworks

Israel has achieved an amount of leisure that is comparable to the amount of leisure of many developed societies. Leisure is not necessarily an asset, however, and people must be taught how to use it wisely. Skills and knowledge for the wise use of leisure are not spontaneously acquired, but must be learned.

It is for the purpose of assisting the educational authorities in Israel to prepare children and youth for the wise use of leisure that the following principles are presented.

The Responsibility of the Public School in Educating for Leisure

Principle 1: The public school, which is the main institution of education having children under its jurisdiction during their formative years, should assume major responsibility in educating for leisure and in initiating leisure preparation for the entire community.

The responsibility of preparing children for leisure-centered living runs throughout the learning experience of the home, school, and other community institutions; however, the school is the most competent institution to prepare children and youth for leisure. As society shifts from a work-centered way of life to a leisure-centered way of life, the public school should assume major responsibility for educating for leisure. The public school has an obligation to educate all ages, both sexes, and all mental, emotional, and physical levels of children and youth under its jurisdiction to their best potentialities. This includes educational activities that inculcate skills, knowledge, attitudes, and interest and provide opportunities in order to achieve educational goals.

The Role of Leisure Education in the Public School

Principle 2: The program of leisure education in the public school should be regarded as an end in itself, with its own values for free growth and development in recreative activity. Therefore, the program should be formally recognized and implemented as a separate goal of public, primary, and post-primary education.

The public school should view education for the wise use of leisure as equal in importance to vocational preparation, and should therefore assume full responsibility for the integration of leisure education within its aims and curricula. Children and youth must be educated in competencies for avocations as well as vocations. Education for the wise use of leisure is not just supplementary education, but rather part and parcel for the educational program. All educational activities in the school should be regarded as equal in importance.

The Goals of Leisure Education
Principle 3: The program of leisure education in the public school should assist children and youth in achieving the good life and the wise use of leisure through the cultivation of their personal intellectual, moral, physical, and social development.

In a leisure-centered society, people seek the good life mainly during leisure, through the pursuit of happiness. Leisure that is used wisely is an opportunity for the achievement and enhancement of the good life. The achievement of this should be the ultimate goal of public education.

The Objectives of Leisure Education
Principle 4: In order to achieve the goals of leisure education the public school should prepare children and youth: *a)* to judge values and select those which are the highest and most durable; *b)* to choose and evaluate leisure activities; *c)* to determine goals and standards for leisure behavior; and *d)* to be aware of and understand the importance and scope of the wise use of leisure in a leisure-centered society.

This preparation should develop a well-rounded person who has attitudes, interests, motivations, habits, knowledge, appreciations, and skills that are usable throughout life.

The Content of the Program of Leisure Education
Principle 5: The program of leisure education should prepare children to reach the good life and the wise use of leisure through leisure expressions that have the potential to contribute to the intellectual, aesthetic, social, and physical development of the individual as well as through his preparation for relaxing during leisure.

Many school experiences are rich in potential for providing leisure education. Everything the student does in school under educational control may contribute to his attitudes, knowledge, habits, and skills in the wise use of leisure. Intellectual development can be achieved through reading, study of literature, language, and science, and involvement in various intellectual hobbies. Aesthetic appreciation can be approached through involvement in and study of music, painting, dance, and drama. Social development can be attained through participation in team games, school clubs, and community service. Physical development can be achieved through exercises, games and sports, outdoor living, dance, hobbies of a physical nature, and safety and survival activities. Desirable relaxation can be achieved through enlightening the pupil about methods of contemplation, reflection, and repose, indoors as well as outdoors.

Most school subjects can and should contribute to leisure education. This can be achieved by emphasizing their value and potential for preparation for leisure. All school experiences should be explored in order to determine their potential contribution to building favorable approaches to leisure.

Principle 6: The program of leisure education should provide experiences that assure personal development of the individual and cultural development of the society through creative expressions that, on their highest level, reach the form of art. These should include creative outlets in aesthetic pursuits that enable one to actively create something in line, form, color, sound, or graceful use of the body. They should also assure that pupils will find pleasure in what others do in all forms of art.

Creative activities provide opportunities for self-expression, for achievement, and for immediate as well as lasting satisfactions that stem from creative effort. Leisure education should include activities that develop the ability to recognize beauty and that provide extensive opportunities for the development of creative skills. Creative activities in communicative human expressions—reading, creative writing, appreciation of literature, conversations, and listening—have implications for leisure, and so are all forms of art. Music is a form of special importance that can become a means of personal satisfaction, of group identification, and of opening channels into broad human relations during leisure. Through dance, rhythm, and drama, people are able to express themselves in a creative and artistic way. All these are human expressions that condition the development of the individual and the culture of the society.

Principle 7: The program of leisure education should provide leisure experiences that contribute to a person's social development through expressions of companionship, belonging, and cooperative group expression. These should include mainly recreational expressions that provide opportunities for primary group associations.

In Israeli society, which is characterized by various ethnic groups, there is preservation to some degree of certain cultural and recreational patterns of leisure behavior. Recreational activities tend to cause intermingling of patterns of leisure behavior, however, and in this way contribute to the cultural integration of the nation.

Principle 8: Although a program of leisure education should stimulate participation in and respect for various patterns of leisure behavior of various ethnic groups, its main concern should be the enhancement of leisure experiences that cause intermingling of patterns of leisure behavior in order to promote cultural integration and social cohesion.

The process of assimilating the masses of new immigrants to Israel who have come from different environments and cultures, and the efforts of the country to integrate all ethnic groups into one unified and homogeneous nation, requires a corresponding adjustment of the program of leisure education to these specific needs. The program must assist acculturation and integration during leisure. A reduction in heterogeneity of cultural traditions and a creation of a unified nation can be enhanced by such leisure pursuits as the study and reading of the Bible, interest in archaeology, trips, hobbies, and other leisure activities that center on the search for national identity.

Principle 9: The program of leisure education should provide recreational activities that offer opportunities for social associations of members of the family, in order to promote social cohesion and solidarity of the family.

Recreational social activities of children and parents that are sponsored by the school enable members of the family to play together or to participate together in various leisure pursuits. Such efforts to integrate pupils and parents in mutual community recreation programs promote family solidarity as well as the cohesion of the community as a whole.

Principle 10: The program of leisure education for urban

children and youth should provide opportunities to acquire the skills, attitudes, and appreciations necessary for the enjoyment of the outdoors. The program should lead to involvement in leisure hobbies and leisure pursuits that are based upon the organic and biological resources and natural environment of the country and that satisfy a person's physical well-being and solitude in leisure.

In an urban society like Israel's, children and youth must be aware of the potential of the outdoors through such experiences as camping and outdoor education. The small size of the country, the mild weather, the variety of natural resources in Israel, and the easy access to them underscore the importance of outdoor pursuits within the program of leisure education. The activities of the Youth Corps in postprimary school should enhance preparation for outdoor living by placing an emphasis upon the development of skills and knowledge related to outdoor recreation pursuits.

Whatever can best be learned in the outdoors, through direct experience of nature, should be approached there. Outdoor education should enrich leisure programs through experiences in and for the outdoors. It should encourage social living, provide work experiences, offer appreciation and knowledge of nature, and develop recreational skills in the outdoors.

Principle 11: The program of leisure education should provide physical activity that will contribute to healthful living through the skillful use of the body. This physical activity can be achieved through physical education and its associated activities, such as intramural and interscholastic athletics. These should contribute to the wise use of leisure through the provision of opportunities to acquire skills and knowledge in physical activities.

People have activity drives and need physical activity in order to maintain healthful living. The skillful use of the body stimulates the individual to participate in physical activity during leisure. The school must provide big-muscle activity, especially in an era of automation when such activity is not met during work time. Both Israel's entry into the era of automation and the changing patterns of occupation stress the sedentary nature of existence; therefore, physical recreation elements during leisure should be emphasized.

Principle 12: Since curricular and extracurricular physical activities are favored by many children and adolescents, special attention should be given to their content and conduct. These activities should include a wide variety of games and sports that have carry-over values to the pupil's future leisure as well as those which satisfy his interest during school years. Activities of a social, coeducational, individual and, dual nature should be included.

Principle 13: The over-all program should be oriented in such a way as to assure the extension of professional leadership and existing facilities to all students and to avoid emphasizing the excellence of the few to the neglect of the many.

Principle 14: The program of leisure education should assure the development of sufficient inner resources in the individual to enable him to spend part of his time in solitude, either in contemplation or in other worthwhile activities that will prevent boredom or dissatisfaction with himself and provide a way of relaxation and self-realization. The individual should be taught not to depend entirely upon company or diversion. Hobbies, reading, writing, and manual arts of all kinds are types of activities that should be particularly valuable for the individual pupil who wants to be alone during leisure.

Principle 15: The program of leisure education should encourage all children and youth to regard worship as an essential human need and should motivate them to fully respect devotion to this human expression by others and to be fully aware of ways of enjoying leisure pursuits without interfering with the worship of others.

The effect of orthodox Jewish religion in Israel upon the use of leisure cannot be ignored, and it must be taken into consideration in order to achieve national integration.

Principle 16: The program of leisure education should provide for the inculcation of a balanced approach to relaxation as an important aspect of leisure. Pupils should know how to relax properly not only through sleep and inactivity, but also through activities that have the potential to offset mental fatigue.

Each pupil should know how to achieve a proper balance between activity and inactivity during leisure. Pursuits of quiet or passive recreation that involve viewing, listening, or contemplation can serve effectively as forms of relaxation.

Principle 17: The program of leisure education should provide leisure experiences that satisfy the needs and interests of children and youth and prevent antisocial behavior, especially of the adolescent.

Greater attention to the play life of children and youth should be given. Leisure becomes the center of life for most pupils, and the use of this leisure may become socially acceptable or socially unacceptable. Since the school age is a most fruitful time in a person's growth, special, more intensive, and more extensive attention to the preparation for recreative leisure should be given. Opportunities to meet the special needs of teenagers, such as the need for individualism and adventure, should be provided through creative, social, cultural, and recreational experiences that may prevent juvenile delinquency and other misuses of leisure.

Principle 18: The program of leisure education should provide special experiences for girls that are adjusted to their needs and interests and will prepare them adequately for the wise use of their future leisure as women, within and outside the home.

The increase in discretionary time available to women due to technological advances underscores the need to educate young girls for the wise use of leisure. Girls should be prepared for a variety of semileisure activities, such as sewing, knitting, and gardening, as well as for pure leisure activities, such as various creative and cultural hobbies and for engagement in social service and community activities.

Principle 19: The program of leisure education should consider the needs of the handicapped who cannot participate in the regular program unless it is specially adapted for them.

All pupils who are physically or mentally handicapped

should be prepared to enjoy leisure. The program should adjust activities to fit the individual needs and requirements of these pupils, whether they are in separate specialized schools or in a regular school setting. The treatment or correction of certain physical and mental defects should be considered an important function of the school, as should the provision of a broad recreational program, properly supervised and adapted to the physical and mental needs of atypical pupils. Such a program should prepare these pupils to live a happier life during leisure.

Educational Channels for Leisure Education

Principle 20: Curricular subjects that have the potential to contribute to the wise use of leisure should be specifically designed to educate for leisure through particular units of instruction and defined attainments.

A careful analysis of each subject area in the school curriculum should be performed in order to discover its potential contribution as a leisure activity. Avocational values of subjects such as social education, manual and handicrafts studies, physical education, nature and science, music education, Bible education, language, arithmetic, and geography should be emphasized. Topics and units within each subject can be suggested as desirable educational means of preparing for the wise use of leisure.

Principle 21: The program of leisure education should include experiences beyond the classroom that should be regarded as an integral part of the educational process of the school. These should include informal and voluntary cocurricular, extracurricular, and supplementary educational activities for all children, both in primary and postprimary school, which contribute to the achievement of leisure education goals. An emphasis should be placed on forms of play and recreation that are spontaneous, enjoyable, and provide opportunities for self-expression during leisure that may become lifetime hobbies.

Informal and voluntary experiences beyond the classroom should offer a wide variety of opportunities for self-expression in meaningful and worthwhile activities. They should afford freedom of choice, which permits the discovery of one's special capacities and interests, and should assure spontaneity and enjoyment in leisure participation.

Principle 22: Guidance activities that lead the pupils toward self-direction and self-realization for the wise use of leisure should be included in the program of leisure education.

The school should serve as a guidance agency for avocational interests. Guidance services that aim to assisting in the preparation of children and youth for the wise use of leisure should be provided by every primary and postprimary school, preferably by teachers who have an adequate background in recreation and guidance techniques. This educational process can persuade each pupil to learn many kinds of leisure activities and to develop special interests in several. It can also show the potential importance of various pursuits.

Desirable Characteristics of the Program of Leisure Education

Principle 23: The program of leisure education should include activities that have the potential to be chosen voluntarily during leisure and should encourage voluntary participation in as many activities as possible.

Leisure is time available for spontaneous choosing, while recreation is one major activity chosen for such available time. Leisure education should influence and condition voluntary participation through values, appreciations, skills, attitudes and knowledge that the pupil acquires in primary and postprimary school. The pupil should be provided with the means to enable him to choose to use leisure according to his personal tastes. Voluntary expression is present in most forms of recreational activities; therefore, these should be part and parcel of leisure education.

Principle 24: The program of leisure education should provide adequate opportunities for each individual pupil to utilize his unique talents; however, it should not place any emphasis upon the individual's excellence or upon his level of achievement.

It should be recognized that each child is unique and should be considered as such in the development of the program. Since people vary in their range of interests, the program should offer a wide choice of activities that may arouse and sustain the particular interest of each child. Too much attention to special individual talents, however, may lead to an emphasis on excellence that should be avoided in the public school setting. In such a setting, a balance between attention to the individual child and equal attention to all children should be maintained.

Principle 25: The program of leisure education should recognize and consider human characteristics at various stages of life. Experiences that possess carry-over values into adult life in all forms of leisure expression should be provided, in order to effectively prepare for the wise use of leisure.

What children and youth acquire during their formative years will determine their future leisure activities; therefore, as many as possible of the activities provided in the leisure education program should be of a nature that enables pupils to adopt them as lifetime pursuits. There are many activities that can be carried on into adult life while satisfying the interests and needs of both children and adults, and these should play a major role in the program. The cooperative efforts of the school's leisure education program and the program of community recreation may enhance the carry-over of skills acquired in school into the lives of workers and the aged.

Principle 26: The program of leisure education should provide varied and balanced activity that will expose children and youth to as many leisure expressions as possible, in order to help them to discover their own field of interest, make desirable choices, and provide for varied, balanced, and healthful living.

Education for leisure should place emphasis on balance. The pupil should be encouraged to familiarize himself with many leisure activities in order to become proficient in as many as possible. This exposure to a variety of activities assures his harmonious growth. Such activities should include physical, social, aesthetic, creative, and outdoor activities and hobbies. No emphasis should be placed on the development of proficiency in one leisure expression only. Although emphasis should be placed upon the foregoing activities, pupils should also be exposed to other leisure expressions, such as solitude and diversion. However, these should be encouraged within the general framework of balanced and varied recreational pursuits.

Principle 27: The program of leisure education should take into consideration different climatic conditions, and should therefore provide indoor as well as outdoor activities that are suitable for various seasons of the year.

It should be realized that there are possibilities for continuous and year-round leisure education. Climatic conditions in Israel and seasonal fluctuations in temperature affect leisure, and should therefore be considered in the program of leisure education. Indoor activities should be provided during rainy and cold weather as well as on extremely hot summer days. However, due to the mild climatic conditions generally prevailing in Israel, the program should emphasize outdoor activity.

Principle 28: The program of leisure education should anticipate and eliminate all possible hazards to health and physical well-being that may often occur in various leisure activities.

The mental and physical well-being of the pupils can be improved by the wise use of leisure through play and recreation. These expressions contribute to a person's well-being and prevent mental and physical problems; however, various play and recreation activities have the potential for aggravating such problems. Physical hazards, such as the use of inadequate facilities and equipment, and mental hazards, such as excessive excitement and competitiveness, should be avoided.

Educational and Administrative Methods of Leisure Education

Principle 29: Experiences within the program of leisure education in the school should be taught through informal as well as formal teaching methods, in which the leader inspires, sets examples, stimulates, and guides rather than dictates.

Although leisure experiences can and should be taught compulsorily, they should not be taught autocratically. A play spirit should be included in the teaching of leisure skills and knowledge. Less emphasis should be placed upon highly organized and formal leisure programs. The pupils should have a part in determining their needs and interests and planning the program, and the program should be carried out, as far as possible, in the voluntary and free atmosphere that characterizes leisure.

Principle 30: The classroom teacher in the primary school and the specialist in the postprimary school should have a background of leisure education that includes aspects of cultural, social, artistic, and athletic leisure pursuits. This background should be constantly maintained and improved.

All teachers in the public school should be fully aware of the vital role of leisure in a modern industrial society and of its educational implications for the social welfare of the nation and the well-being of the individual pupil. At the professional training level, courses interpreting the implications of leisure for education should be given. Education for leisure should be given more consideration by teachers, who should be oriented to the view that it is their responsibility to prepare children for avocations as well as vocations.

Principle 31: In order to improve cocurricular activities, the leaders and instructors of these activities should be recognized as professionals who are regular members of the school staff, and their training should be comparable at least to the level of teacher preparation.

Principle 32: In order to assure a proper program of leisure education for all pupils, the public school should provide adequate resources to satisfy the instructional needs of various recreational activities.

The school should develop its physical resources for leisure education, and it should be planned, designed, and used for leisure purposes.

Principle 33: The program of leisure education should utilize all material and human resources within and outside the school. It should make maximal use of facilities for various leisure activities in order to enrich their educational possibilities.

The program planner should consider all available facilities, space, and equipment. Improvisation and imagination can often be used if facilities and equipment are lacking. All available resources for the use of leisure education should be made known to the planner, including the facilities of private and public agencies, schools, and parks. The extent of the program will be conditioned by the resources available for each particular activity. The maximal use of resources can be enhanced by using modern means of transportation to facilitate access to resources outside the school.

Principle 34: The public school should base its program of leisure education on the cooperative efforts of the school and other community institutions and should coordinate its leisure education program with the community.

The school is a community institution that should have an interest in the overall welfare of the community and should therefore initiate and plan leisure preparation and pursuits for the community as a whole. Coordination of school and community programs for the wise use of leisure will enhance the school's efforts to educate children and youth. Cooperative planning of recreational facilities and mobilization of total community resources for leisure education will contribute to the enrichment and effectiveness of the program.

Principle 35: Special attention should be devoted in Israel to cooperation between the public schools and the youth movements. Leisure education should be enhanced through reciprocal efforts that provide school and recreational resources for the youth movements and that introduce the unique, informal approach of the youth movements into the school's extracurricular activities.

Principle 36: The postprimary school system in Israel, especially the vocational school, should broaden its program of instruction to include not only the traditional academic subjects and occupational skills but also the knowledge and skills needed for a leisure-centered society.

In the postprimary school, after-school and extracurricular programs should provide the main leisure experiences; however, these experiences should be enhanced by curricular and guidance activities. Special emphasis should be laid on leisure education in the vocational schools, which are almost completely lacking in opportunities for leisure education. The postprimary school can no longer content itself with the function of implanting theoretical and vocational knowledge, leaving education for leisure to the home, the youth movement, or some other outside agency. Development of skills and knowledge for leisure education must form an integral part of the postprimary school.

Principle 37: The program of leisure education should be subject to continuous evaluation, which will assure desirable changes and an adequate adjustment to developments in the quantity and quality of leisure.

The lives of people in Israel are influenced by various factors creating leisure and by other factors affecting leisure. The effects of these factors change rapidly and with them, the quantity and quality of leisure. Standards of living and cultural standards and values may be different in the future for various groups in Israeli society. Thus, the ways and means by which the wise use of leisures by all groups of "leisurites" can be achieved should be subject to continuous reevaluation.

SOURCES

American Association for Health, Physical Education, and Recreation. *School Recreation*. Washington, D.C.: AAHPER, 1960.

Brightbill, C. K. *Educating for Leisure Centered Living*. Harrisburg, Pa.: Stackpole Co., 1966.

Hutchinson, J. L. *Leisure and the Schools*. Washington, D.C.: AAHPER, 1961.

Jenny, J. H. *Introduction to Recreation Education*. Philadelphia: W. B. Saunders Co., 1955.

Krauss, R. G. *Recreation and the Schools*. New York: Macmillan Co., 1964.

Murdy, J., and Odum L. *Leisure Education: Theory and Practice*. New York: John Wiley & Sons, 1979.

Ruskin, H. Principles for Leisure Education in the Public Schools of Israel. Ph.D. thesis, New York University, 1968.

Wylie, J. A. "Education for Leisure" *Journal of Education*, October 1960, pp. 1–67.

Political and Philosophical Implications Arising from a Public Education Campaign: The Canadian Experience

Saul Ross

Eternal vigilance is the price of liberty.
Attributed to Thomas Jefferson

Canadian Political Organization and Structure

Canada is a land of paradoxes and contrasts. Located in the northern half of the North American continent, it is the world's second-largest country (only the USSR is larger); but with its population of approximately 25 million, it is one of the smallest nations. Eight percent of the population inhabits 10 percent of the land, a narrow band running along the border with the United States. Largely urban despite vast expanses of farmland, Canada's two major cities, Toronto and Montreal, contain approximately 25 percent of the population.

French adventurers were the first Europeans to explore and settle permanently in what we now call North America. In pursuit of the fur trade, they ventured into the heart of the continent, establishing a string of settlements and forts stretching from Quebec down along the Mississippi River to New Orleans.[1] English explorers and settlers followed, arriving first in the south and then gradually spreading out.

This added another arena in the eighteenth-century rivalry

Saul Ross, Ph.D. is associate professor, Department of Physical Education, University of Ottawa, Canada.

between England and France. The Seven Years' War (1756–63) fought between these two "world powers" ended with the signing of the Treaty of Paris, whereby New France was ceded to England.

From 1763 to 1840, a number of forms of government were tried, each one moving closer to self-government.[2] Prodded by a variety of internal and external factors,[3] the concept of a union of British North America was an idea whose time had come in the 1860s. On a petition from the provincial colonies, the British Parliament, in 1867, passed legislation entitled the British North America Act, bringing about Canada's independence by evolution.

Though it is often referred to as our constitution, the BNA Act is in fact not a constitution at all in the sense of the American constitution. It is the formal instrument of union and contains explicit definitions of large areas of Canadian government.[4] Section 91 enumerates the jurisdictional powers of the Parliament of Canada, and Section 92 lists the exclusive powers of the provincial legislatures. In their wisdom, the framers of the BNA Act endowed the federal government with most of the taxation powers, but allocated the social responsibilties to the provinces, thereby setting the stage for continuing tension and cooperation between the two levels of government.

Confederation came into effect 1 July 1867. It was the product of several years of negotiations—among the colonies first and then with Britain. The BNA Act is founded on the British system of parliamentary government, whose tradition the provinces had inherited and on which their own political institutions were modeled, although modified to suit local needs. When considering the form of federal government, the founding fathers looked also to the experience of the United States and adopted a number of features from the neighbor to the south. "The combining of the British parliamentary system with the American federal principles was a symbolic achievement—all the more so when both elements were freely adapted to Canada's own particular needs."[5]

Two points are pertinent to the topic at hand. First, throughout her history Canada has been pulled in two directions by geography and tradition.[6] Geographically, our proximity to the United States is obvious; we share a 4,000-mile unguarded border. In addition, the natural geographic lines run north and south in contradiction to the political realities, which run east and west. This geographic proximity, combined with the wealth and productivity of the United States, has a direct impact on Canadians. Most movies, books, magazines, and other culture-shaping media in Canada are really products of another country, another society. The American influence is counterbalanced, in part, by the European, particularly the French and British, heritage.[7]

Second, both influences, American and British, are those of Western, liberal democracy. Civil liberties, personal rights, and the freedom of the individual are paramount values. Canada, in its traditional role, occupies a middle position between the social welfare democracy of England and the "rugged individualism" form of democracy found in the United States.

A Social Revolution

Medicare—a form of government-legislated, universal medical insurance—is not a new concept, as it dates back to the last century when Chancellor Bismarck introduced it in Germany.[8] In Canada, the idea was first introduced in the 1920s and promptly put in abeyance.

During the federal election in 1963, Lester B. Pearson, then leader of the Liberal party, emphasized the urgency of enacting a health insurance plan. This was one of the major planks in the Liberal platform. The Liberals were elected, and shortly after taking power they appointed a royal commission under the chairmanship of the distinguished jurist, Mr. Justice Emmett Hall, to determine how best to implement such a scheme.

Following the report of the royal commission, Bill C-227, the Medical Care Bill, was introduced into parliament on 29 June 1966, given first reading on 12 July, and passed on 21 December 1966. Officially, it carries the title Medical Care

Act and came into effect 1 July 1967, on Canada's centennial celebration. A cost-sharing formula (50–50) was negotiated between the federal government and the provinces to pay for the program. Universal coverage, accessibility, and portability are integral components, or basic tenets, of the Medical Care Act. Passage of the legislation and solutions found to the federal-provincial jurisdictional differences meant that as of 1 July 1967, Canada entered a new era with regard to medical care. From that date, all medical facilities, services, and resources became available to all Canadians. An individual's financial status was no longer a factor in determining the level and amount of medical service he would receive.

An Ensuing Problem

During the parliamentary debate on Bill C-227, many aspects were discussed, ranging from pure partisan political posturing to well-researched, serious, probing comments. One comment, made by D. R. Gundlock, M. P., showed clear foresight and presaged the development of an aspect of medicare that is pertinent here.

I would quote a very, very eminent English surgeon who four months before the medicare bill was introduced in his country had a waiting list of 65, and five months after it was introduced he had a waiting list of 365.[9]

Mr. Gundlock's example focuses on the increased work load for physicians, but it also demonstrates that under medicare more people avail themselves of medical services more often, resulting in a phenomenal increase in cost.

During the six-year period 1968–73, collective federal, provincial and local governments' expenditure on health more than doubled, expanding from $2,665.2 million to $6,069.4 million. When adjusted for population growth, per capita expenditure on health was over twice as much in 1973 as in 1968, namely $270 compared with $127.[10]

These data must be considered within the context of the following statement: "Canada spends more of its GNP on health care than any other Western country—5.2 percent in 1969 (this compares to 4.7 percent in the U.S. and 3.6 percent in Britain for the same year)."[11,12] According to one source, costs were "growing at a rate of about 13 percent a year, 50 percent faster than the economy generally. The total bill is expected to triple in the next ten years."[13]

With costs rising so quickly, wild predictions were made—projections based on an extrapolation of available data indicated that by the year 2000 Canada's total GNP could be committed to medicare, an obviously untenable situation.

Discounting the hysteria and hyperbole, a serious problem still faced the elected politicians. Seemingly, all measures that could be prescribed for stanching the increase were politically unpalatable. Deterrent fees impose an extra tax on low-income people, the very group that was to benefit most from medicare. Excluding some categories of service means alienating various segments of the population—professionals as well as people who need that particular service. Imposing a fee for services beyond a basic limit means adding a financial burden to people who are already in a very stressful situation. It seemed that ideas such as those just mentioned, either where additional specific costs were imposed or where some category of service or illness was excluded, detracted from the basic concept of universal medical care and hence had to be rejected.

At about this very time, interest in physical fitness emerged as a major topic of interest and concern among such organizations as university physical education departments, YMCAs and YMHAs, and the Fitness and Amateur Sport Directorate of the federal Department of Health and Welfare.

Canada in the 1960s was a nation of spectators. A study commissioned by the Fitness and Amateur Sport Directorate and conducted by a prominent consulting firm, P. S. Ross,[14] revealed that adult Canadians spent as much as 85 percent of their leisure time in passive activities, such as watching television or driving a car. More time was spent watching television than all other leisure-time activities combined. Another study, conducted by Ben Crow and Associates,[15] disclosed that less than 2 percent of the Canadian population participated in physical activities as frequently as once a week. Additional data are available to support these findings.[16]

Hypokinesis, a term that refers to a syndrome that results from lack of activity, aptly describes Canadians at that period. Lack of participation in sports and physical activities results in low levels of physical fitness, a condition deemed troublesome: people in poor physical condition appear to need more medical services. Perhaps the solution to stemming the rising medicare costs lay in prevention: that is, if some way could be found to raise the fitness level of all, or most, Canadians, then the concomitant improvement in health would reduce the need for medical services and ergo stanch the continuing escalation in medical costs.

Sports Participation Canada—Participaction

The headline of an article in the *Montreal Star* on 22 January 1972, which announced the founding of Sports Participation Canada, states, "Waist Land: Canada going to pot [alongside the headline is a picture of a distended male stomach]. New fitness group wants to get nation on its feet."[17] The overwhelming inactivity of Canadians is a major concern; Sports Participation Canada is out to change this state of affairs.

Phillipe de Gaspe Beaubien, a prominent Canadian business executive who was instrumental in developing Sports Participation Canada, points to the data cited above regarding lack of participation as the motivation that sparked his efforts.[18] In Beaubien's view, Canadians tend to reward sickness and disability rather than try to prevent it. "There is not enough emphasis on the economic and social benefits of good health. We are a nation of sitters and spectators."[19] Sports Participation Canada, which soon adopted the catchy word *Participaction*, was formed to change the Canadian way of life.

An examination of the confidential document entitled "Proposal for the Establishment and Funding of a Private Non-

Profit Company to Increase Mass Participation in Sports, Physical Recreation and Fitness Activities"[20] reveals that mass persuasion is the basic doctrine of the formation of Participaction. The proposal has an introductory section titled "Problems," in which the lack of participation is noted and the belief expressed that increased participation in physically active games and sports has a marked positive effect on physical and mental health. Next comes a statement that "organized persuasion [i.e., propaganda] is vital to increasing participation."[21]

A sports communication's enterprise is proposed whose function it would be "to improve the well-being of Canadians by persuading them to increase their participation in sports, physical recreation and fitness activities."[22] Providing more facilities or additional programs was regarded as insufficient— attitudes must be changed. Citing the work of Kahn and Weiner *(The Year 2000)* and the twelve-part series in the *Monetary Times* by John Kettle entitled "2000," the proposal maintains that unless leisure is properly developed, it is a threat to the social structure and stability as we know it.[23] In brief, the prospects are that unless attitudes are changed, an increase in leisure time will only aggravate the present imbalance against sports, physical activity, fitness, and well-being.

Searching about for alternatives, one idea was proposed and then discarded:

> The idea of developing Sports-Communication as an activity within the new agency, Information Canada, came to mind. However, this was decided to be unsuitable for the overriding reason that the new activity would require the use of techniques of outright propaganda, something which Information Canada has been disavowing since its formation.[24]

Information Canada, as a unit within the Department of Supply and Services, came into existence 1 April 1970. When the government first announced its formation, many voices were raised in protest at what appeared to be an intrusion on the democratic process, namely, the government using taxpayers' dollars to disseminate propaganda. The government replied that Information Canada would confine itself to the distribution and sale of official government documents and other publications not usually handled by bookstores. As a result of financial constraints and government cutbacks, Information Canada was phased out in April 1976.

Based on the data presented, the arguments marshaled, and the alternatives examined, a proposal was made "to incorporate a non-profit private company whose object would be to increase sports participation through persuasion."[25]

Sports Participation Canada came into being in September 1971 as a nonprofit, private company with the Right Honorable Lester B. Pearson as chairman of the board and Phillipe de Gaspe Beaubien as president. A board of directors, such as is found in industry, was appointed to guide the company. Since its inception, in accordance with the original proposal,[26] there has always been federal government representation on the board. A small full-time staff with strong marketing skills was hired.

Funding for this nonprofit, private company came from the federal government. A $350,000 grant from the Fitness and Amateur Sport Directorate was regarded as seed money with the eventual goal being self-sufficiency as involvement from the private sector increased.

Sports Participation Canada set about publicizing itself and informing Canadians of its objective, namely, "to increase the physical fitness level of all Canadians by convincing them of the need for more physical activity."[27] In another pamphlet they describe their assignment: "To promote improved physical activity and physical fitness in the average Canadian."[28] A clear statement is provided of how they plan to achieve their objective:

> We're going to get Canadians up. We're going to show them that being physically fit can give a whole new lease on life. We'll tease, tempt, coax, and wheedle; induce, seduce, attract, persuade, lure, prod, challenge, entreat, inspire, and conspire to get Canadians up and moving, and when we get them moving, we're going to keep them moving. It's going to be quite a ride.[29]

In a letter to his fellow members of the Canadian Association for Health, Physical Education and Recreation, Russ Kisby, national coordinator, detailed the three-step marketing method to be used by Participaction:

1. If we look at physical activity as a new consumer product to be marketed, we would want to first try to convince the market that the product is needed. This will be the *motivational* part of our campaign.
2. The next step in a marketing strategy is to show consumers where and how they get the product. This is the *solution* part of the campaign.
3. The third step is to offer constant reminders as to why consumers should keep using the product. This we will call, surprisingly enough, the *reminder* portion of the campaign.[30]

Increased sports participation, which should result in higher levels of fitness, is the goal; persuasion, in the form of social marketing, is the method to be employed.

Today, Participaction operates in accordance with the philosophy enunciated in the original proposal. This basic concept, whether it is labeled persuasion, propaganda, communication, or social marketing, has been elaborated into a program that has four broad thrusts:

1. Public service advertising via the mass media. Basically, the operating principle is to take government seed money to produce the message and distribute it to the various media who then give Participaction exposure free of charge. Participaction has never paid for any advertising time or space—it has always been 100 percent donated.

Based on current market rates, the value of all advertising has been assessed at $8 million in each of the past two years.

2. Public sector support. Part of the federal government grant is used to create posters, booklets, and leaflets, which are mass-produced to decrease the cost per unit. These items are then sold on a cost-recovery basis to the provincial governments, who overprint their own credits before distribution. The cost of distribution, which is a major expense, is borne by each province.

Federal funds are used originally, but through sales to the provinces this expenditure is eventually recouped and reused for creative purposes.

3. Corporate sponsorship. Creative ideas developed by Participaction to promote fitness are available to corporations who wish to use them as a tie-in with their own advertising campaigns. Participaction provides the creative materials that are designed for a specific corporation, and the message is underwritten as part of the advertising budget. It is a straight business approach in terms of marketing, with part of the message devoted to promoting fitness.

For example, one bank spent $250,000 on a series of posters depicting a variety of fitness activities. The posters were free, but available only in the branches of that bank. In terms of marketing, offering free posters meant increased traffic in each branch, which should translate into more customers. In a very competitive line of business—interest rates and range of services are basically the same in all banks—promoting physical fitness enhances the corporate image of the bank.

4. Promotional merchandising. Some items, such as T-shirts, booklets, and posters, are sold at a small profit, which is returned to the operating budget.

To maximize profits and eliminate the charge of unfair competition, Participaction is involved only in direct sales that they handle themselves. Operating in this manner obviously limits sales. An additional limitation exists. In keeping with its stated goal, Participaction will only consider sales items that are directly related to fitness; i.e., posters, pamphlets, and T-shirts.[31]

Federal funds are used to produce materials which, either independently or in conjunction with other agencies (be they commercial organizations or provincial governments), are designed to persuade Canadians to become more active. Using tax dollars in this manner was an issue alluded to only briefly and tangentially in the original proposal.

Essentially a public relations project, this program, however, because of its involvement with Federal, Provincial and Municipal

Governments, the school systems, private associations and enterprises, and because of the outright techniques of propaganda it
will be using, *can be recognized but should not be publicized as a creation
of the Federal Government.*[32] (Italics mine)

Propaganda is an evocative word that stimulates strong emotional reaction; *social marketing* is a more neutral, less provoca-
tive phrase and the term preferred by Participaction to describe its main function. Social marketing is a relatively new
phenomenon,[33] a product of the 1960s and 1970s. Its emergence at this time is somewhat paradoxical. Just when marketing by business firms was being called to task for supposed
abuses and failures, other kinds of organizations, in particular
nonprofit organizations, had begun to recognize that marketing skills were applicable to their problems.[34]
    As in most academic areas, the experts in the field of mar-
keting cannot all agree on one definition for that term. This
problem is not faced by the layman who understands that
marketing involves buying and selling, or an exchange of
goods, and includes a wide range of activities designed
specifically to promote and enhance both the process and the
product. Since the interest of the consumer extends beyond
the economic and materialistic, this realm can also be served
by marketing, specifically social marketing.

> Social marketing is the design, implementation, and control of
> programs calculated to influence the acceptability of social ideas
> and involves considerations of product planning, pricing, com-
> munication, distribution, and marketing research. . . . Thus, it is
> the explicit use of marketing skills to help translate present social
> action efforts into more effectively designed and communicated
> programs that elicit desired audience response.[35]

Marketing's basic responsibility is to generate a profitable
demand for the firm's productive resources. In order to suc-
ceed, marketing requires proper management, which includes
analysis, planning, implementation, and control of programs
designed to bring about desired exchanges with target audi-
ences. Marketing management examines the wants, attitudes,

and behaviors of potential customers as the basis for designing its merchandising and distribution campaign. A number of well-developed, sophisticated tools and techniques are available to help management in its tasks.[36]

In the world of commerce, "all marketing communications are persuasive in intent; their purpose is to stimulate buying action."[37] In social marketing, all marketing communications are persuasive in intent; their purpose, however, is to stimulate the acceptance of the idea propounded. This concept needs to be considered within the context of the claim made by William Barton:

> Marketing also wields enormous influence upon our goals and values—upon our beliefs and assumptions as to what and how much is good, important, worth doing, or worth working for.[38]

Marketing men are trained to be finely attuned to market needs, product development, pricing and channel issues, and mass communications and promotion techniques, all of which are critical in the social area. Basically, the same principles apply whether marketing a commercial product or a social idea—the target audience must be studied and analyzed; the product must be designed and appropriately and then packaged in a manner that the target audience finds desirable and is willing to purchase.[39]

Marketing has always been an integral part of the business world. Recently its concepts and techniques have been employed in social situations. It is a powerful tool; "in the hands of its best practitioners marketing management is applied behavioural science."[40] Applied behavioral science implies social intervention to modify or alter both thinking and behavior.

Political and Philosophical Implications

Philosophers have speculated endlessly on democracy and freedom; the amount of literature devoted to statements, analyses, or criticism of democratic theory is overwhelming.[41] While the intent here is not to add to the existing overabundance, nor to repeat what is obvious to most people, a short description of the essence of democratic philosophy and practice is necessary before examining the issue of social marketing by Participaction.

"Democracy relates to a social practice in which individual freedom is combined with community participation."[42] The democratic pattern arises out of the age-old dialectic between the dual, and seemingly opposite, goals of freedom and order. Democracy has been defined in the simplest way as government by the people. Abraham Lincoln's phrase— "government of the people, by the people, and for the people"—is a small elaboration.[43] A more comprehensive definition is provided by Sargent;

> It is possible to define democracy broadly as a political system based on:
> 1. The involvement of the citizens, either directly or indirectly, in the making of political decisions, with the majority ruling.
> 2. In a representative democracy, majority rule through periodic elections.
> 3. Some degree of equality among the citizens.
> 4. Some degree of liberty, or some rights maintained by the citizens.[44]

On the whole, there is no uniquely democratic social organization except in the very loose sense that a democratic society must be fairly free and open rather than controlled. Some degree of control is required to maintain order, but in a democratic society the thrust is always toward freedom and openness. This predilection for freedom and openness is central to the liberal tradition, which seeks to find ways and means of loosening whatever restrictions are preventing the individual from reaching the outer boundaries of his particular talents.

> Admitting the existence of limits on individual self-responsibility and rationality, the liberal persists in trying to create the kind of

social setting in which every collective resource is turned toward making personal choice more possible and more effective.[45]

In Zimmerman's analysis of democracy, the key concept is the rule of the majority;[46] implicit in the rule of the majority is the delegation of powers. "In a society in which the people maintain control of their government, assignment of power from individuals to those in authority constitutes a delegation rather than a loss of power."[47] Government is the instrument of the people, not their master.

It was Thomas Jefferson who wrote that governments exist to protect and realize the inalienable rights of man.[48] In a democratic society, the basic function of government is the protection of its citizens—from each other and from external enemies. To provide this, the government enacts legislation, which is rules for the conduct of citizens. Police forces and courts are established to enforce the laws enacted.

Protection is a basic responsibility, but, according to Zimmerman, there is an additional function. "In a democratic society the majority not only has the right to control and direct the power of government, but to use this right to enlarge the freedoms of all."[49]

Liberal democracy recognizes individual responsibility. It is a society in which the greatest scope is given to the individual to decide for himself what is good for him. Government intervention into realms where the individual is able to accept full responsibility is regarded as unwarranted intrusion. Whatever does no damage to the society as a whole or to the individuals within it should be the concern of no one but the individual or individuals involved.[50]

Any discussion of democracy must deal largely with the governmental process, in particular the role of government in the lives of the people. Canada, as stated earlier, occupies a middle position between England and the United States as a Western, liberal democratic society. Freedom of choice by individuals is respected.[51] It behoves us now to raise the issue of whether a government-funded agency, even if it is a private, nonprofit company, is compatible with the philosophical ideals of democracy.

Sports Participation Canada is a private, nonprofit company that was inaugurated in 1971 with a $350,000 grant from the federal government. Since then it has received federal funds annually:

1971–72	$262,000
1972–73	$417,469
1973–74	$294,469
1974–75	$500,000
1975–76	$500,000
1976–77	$500,000
1977–78	$350,000[52]

When the founding of Sports Participation Canada was announced, there was general endorsement of the effort. A diligent search of the literature found only one small voice of dissent. Frank Lowe, a syndicated columnist best known for his gentle humor, wrote on 29 December 1971:

> The purpose of all this is to "lure Canadians out of their easy chairs and onto the playing fields or hiking paths."
> This is government interference of the worst kind.
> Why, I might ask, should my tax money be used to attempt to lure me into doing something I loathe? It has taken years of hard work to allow me to get off the hiking path and into my easy chair.
> Somehow I also believe that my physical shape is of no concern to the government. My financial shape, yes. But my physical shape, no.[53]

Lowe objects to the expenditure of tax dollars to convince the taxpayers to change their way of thinking and to modify their behavior. Interest in the financial status of the citizens is warranted (obviously for the purpose of taxation), but interest in the physical condition, and the attempt to alter leisure-time activities, is regarded as government intrusion into an area of life where the individual is fully capable of making decisions for himself. Lowe objects to the expanding role of government, but does not discuss social marketing, the method selected.

In a democratic society, the thrust is toward freedom and openness and away from control. Social marketing is a powerful tool of persuasion; its goal is to convince the target audience—in this case the population of Canada—to accept and adopt an idea. Is the use of social marketing a means of limiting freedom and openness? Is it a subtle mechanism for controlling the people? Within the liberal democratic tradition, where the emphasis is on more choice, the use of social marketing appears to be a move to limit choice and hence may be regarded, in a small way, as detracting from the democratic ideal.

Government enacts legislation, which becomes the rules of conduct for the citizens. These rules are usually clearly stated and explicit—what is prohibited and what is permitted is spelled out in detail. Each citizen should have a clear understanding of what he is permitted to do, which serves to clarify his relationship to the government and to his fellow citizens. The enacted legislation is open to scrutiny, and each citizen is able to form his own opinion regarding its validity and feasibility. At the next election, by casting his ballot, he expresses his judgment. This fundamental democratic process cannot be invoked with regard to the use of social marketing.

It must be made perfectly clear that the importance and desirability of improving the level of fitness of Canadians is not disputed, nor is the efficient fulfillment of its task by Sports Participation Canada under examination. The issue raised is whether a democratic government should ever be involved in social marketing, even when a matter as important as improving the health of the people is involved.

Two aspects of this concern merit further discussion. First, remembering that although there are direct links (funding and representation on the board) between the government and Sports Participation Canada, this aspect was not to be advertised. Would it not have been more in keeping with the concept of responsible government for the government to announce that it was embarking on a campaign itself, using social marketing, to improve the fitness level of Canadians? One of its own departments, such as Fitness Canada or Recreation Canada, could have been given the task. Such an announcement and course of action would have provided the population, the mass media, and the opposition parties with a clear statement of intent and would have allowed for direct questioning of both the goal and the means to be employed in reaching that goal.

Second, by suppressing the connection between the government and Sport Participation Canada, has the government resorted to a form of subterfuge to achieve its goal? Sports Participation Canada is a private, nonprofit organization, but it receives a major ongoing annual grant from the federal government and has federal government representation on its board of directors. Is it a private, nonprofit organization, or is it an extention of the government, even though it is supposedly at "arms length"?

In the original proposal a caution was expressed. Due to the use of outright propaganda techniques, the link between government and Sports Participation Canada was not to be publicized. There is no indication that this information was to be suppressed; it just would not be talked about. That advice has been followed; and while there are a number of people who are aware of the situation—mainly academics and civil servants—they are not the common vehicles for spreading information to the public.

Sports Participation Canada was started with a government grant; its founding was not the result of an act of Parliament. In a democratic society, power is delegated to those elected, and the use or abuse of this trust becomes an issue at the next election. Since the government did not enact legislation to establish Sports Participation Canada, it was not part of the legislative record open to scrutiny during the ensuing election. With regard to delegation of power, it is difficult to envisage a mature, responsible electorate delegating to the government the authority to establish agencies—be they private, nonprofit companies or government departments—whose sole purpose it is to persuade or influence thinking through the use of social marketing. It is equally difficult to envisage the electorate approving a scheme whereby their own tax dollars would be used to create a mechanism designed to persuade them to modify their thinking and alter their behavior.

Improving the level of fitness of Canadians is an issue that would appear to receive wide support. Is this support unanimous? Once a private, nonprofit company has been established and funded by the government to persuade the people to improve their fitness by changing their behavior, what is there then to discourage or prevent the government from repeating the same procedure with regard to other issues? What constitutes consensus or widespread support? How is this consensus or support to be determined? Taken to the extreme, the real concern is that the government might employ social marketing to convince the population to continue reelecting it.

Government tends to amass more power into itself; unless checked it will invade all areas of life. In a democratic society, the challenge is to continue limiting this aggrandizement. Social marketing, whether used directly by government or through an arms-length company, can be regarded as a tool for such aggrandizement. Use of social marketing in this manner can also be regarded as an attempt to reduce freedom of decision, which is contrary to the democratic ideal of maximizing freedom of decision.

Although a democratic society can be distinguished by its primary objective, freedom in community, "it must also be evaluated in terms of present practice. The democratic purpose must be pursued in good faith; it must be demonstrated through tangible effort."[54] Is government-sponsored social marketing a means that is compatible with this democratic ideal?

One of the most fundamental concepts of democracy— freedom—is expressed succinctly by Zimmerman:

> Freedom deserves to be nourished and protected as an end in itself. It is not enough to protect those freedoms implicit in majority rule or those which make up our constitutional rights. It is

essential to widen the range of freedoms humans are capable of experiencing. This constitutes one of the most important goals of a democratic society. This is, in part, what is meant by freedom of the individual.[55]

Government-sponsored or -supported social marketing does not support and enhance the goals expressed by Zimmerman; social marketing has the opposite effect, that is, a diminution of the freedom of the individual.

Along with the political and philosophical issues raised, there is an ethical aspect that deserves consideration. Some observers, both within the marketing community and outside it, consider marketing unethical.[56] All of marketing cannot be indicted, but with regard to some practices the question of ethics looms large. In a democratic society, not only must the government adhere to the letter and spirit of the law, but through all of its acts it must also give the appearance of scrupulous honesty and ethical behavior that is beyond reproach.

Concluding Comment

Two of the most important and difficult problems of political theory are the determination of goals a society should seek and the arrangement of priorities. They are equally complex and arduous practical political problems. Democracies such as Canada are often faced with a dilemma when attempting to revise priorities or when rearranging goals.

All the data available indicated an extremely low rate and level of participation in physical activities and sports on the part of Canadians. Costs for medicare were rising at an alarming rate. Action was needed to rectify both situations. Based on the belief that an increase in the level of fitness would result in a decrease in the use of medical services, thus bringing about a slower rate of increase in medicare costs, the solution arrived at was the founding of Sports Participation Canada— Participaction. It received a large government grant originally and has been receiving federal funds annually. It has govern-

ment representation on its board of directors, and so while it operates at "arms length" from the government, one must question the relationship.

In a democratic society, the government must remain within the spirit of liberal democracy in terms of respect for the integrity and freedom of the individual. Use of social marketing, even if it is implemented by an arms-length company, seems to be inconsistent with the democratic ideal. Kotler and Zaltman, in their thoughtful treatment of social marketing, raise the issue that "there is a definite possibility that the overt marketing of social objectives will be resented and resisted. There will be charges that it is 'manipulative' and consequently contributes to bringing the society closer to Orwell's 1984."[57] We in Canada are very far from anything approaching Orwell's 1984, nor is Participaction seen as paving the way to that fate. At the same time, however, the propriety of government involvement with anything that can be construed as manipulative must be questioned.

Social marketing as a tool of industry and commerce appears to be acceptable because everyone is aware that industry employs these methods to see its products. The same line of thinking would apply to social agencies that receive no government funds. However, use of social marketing, either directly or indirectly, by government in a democracy is another matter.

Democracy is both hardy and fragile. It is hardy in its ability to withstand stresses and demands in times of war and social crises, provided the people are determined to preserve their freedom. When neglect and lack of concern are present and constant vigilance is absent, then democracy can be very fragile.

How then does the government promote the healthy use of leisure? Perhaps the question to be asked is, Should government be involved in leisure at all—beyond providing facilities?

One final comment is needed to address the question of a theoretical framework within which to mold leisure policy. In a democratic society, one fact that must be considered is respect for the spirit and practice of the democratic ideal.

NOTES

1. E. McInnis, *Canada: A Political and Social History*, rev. and enl. (New York: Holt, Rinehart & Winston, 1963), pp. 17–97.

2. Ibid., pp. 125–286.

3. Ibid., pp. 287ff.

4. A. R. M. Lower, *Colony to Nation: A History of Canada* (Toronto: Longmans, Green & Company, 1964), pp. 327 ff.

5. McInnis, *Canada*, p. 299.

6. J. S. Moir and R. E. Saunders, *Northern Destiny: A History of Canada* (Toronto: J. M. Dent & Sons, 1970) pp. 8–9.

7. F. Cosentino, "Sport in the Land of the Beaver, Eagle, and Bear" (Part 1), CAHPER Journal 44, no. 5 (May–June 1978): 15–17, 40–41.

8. Great Britain, *Hansard's Parliamentary Debates* (Commons), 5th ser., 1 October 1966, p. 8668.

9. Ibid., 24 October 1966, p. 9042.

10. *Canada Year Book*, 1976–77, p. 246.

11. "In Search of Physical Fitness", Royal Bank of Canada *Newsletter* 39, no. 1, 1958.

12. John Munro, minister of Health and Welfare, quoted in Andy O'Brian, "Why is Everybody in Saskatoon Going to Walk around the Block on a Cold Winter Night Next Month?" *Weekend Magazine*, 30 December 1972.

13. *Participaction*, leaflet (undated), p. 3.

14. This study, and its result, is widely quoted. I have made a number of attempts to obtain a copy but to date have not succeeded.

15. The result of this study is widely quoted. I have been unable to obtain a copy.

16. "1972 Survey of Selected Leisure Time Activities," *Statistics Canada Service Bulletin, Education Division* 2, no. 1. The population aged fourteen years and over was surveyed, and 75.7 percent reported zero hours participation per week in sports, while 13.1 percent reported 1–3 hours participation per week.

17. Zoe Bieler, "Waist Land: Canada going to pot," *Montreal Star*, 22 January 1972.

18. Ibid.

19. Ibid.

20. "Proposal for the Establishment and Funding of a Private Non-Profit Company to Increase Mass Participation in Sports, Physical Recreation and Fitness Activities," undated and unsigned. There is some evidence to indicate that the proposal was presented either late in 1970 or early in 1971 and is probably the work of Phillipe de Gaspe Beaubien, in conjunction with some officers of the Fitness and Amateur Sport Directorate.

21. Ibid., p. 1.

22. Ibid., p. 2.

23. Ibid., p. 3.

24. Ibid., p. 4.

25. Ibid., p. 5.

26. Ibid., p. 5.

27. *Participaction*, p. 3.

28. *The Canadian Movement for Personal Fitness: Participaction*, pamphlet published by Sports Participation Canada, 1972.

29. Ibid.

30. Russ Kisby, "Sports Participation Canada," letter sent to all members of the Canadian Association for Health, Physical Education and Recreation, February 1972. See also "Sports Participation Canada: Participaction", CAHPER *Journal* 38, no. 6 (July–August 1972): 10–14.

31. Russ Kisby, president of Participaction, private communication to the author, 7 May 1979.

32. "Proposal for the Establishment," p. 6.

33. W. Lazer and E. J. Kelley, "Social Marketing: A Conceptual Framework," in W. Lazer and E. J. Kelley, eds. *Social Marketing: Perspectives and Viewpoints* (Homewood, Ill.: Richard D. Irwin, 1973), p. 3–4.

34. F. E. Webster, *Social Aspects of Marketing* (Englewood Cliffs, N.J.: Prentice-Hall, 1974), p. 1.

35. P. Kotler and G. Zaltman, "Social Marketing: An Approach to Planned Social Change," *Journal of Marketing* 35 (July 1971): 5.

36. One example can be found in the systems approach proposed by M. Hanan in his book, *Life-Styled Marketing* (New York: American Management, 1972), p. 3. Another approach is found in Kotler and Zaltman, "Social Marketing," pp. 10,11.

37. Webster, *Social Aspects of Marketing*, p. 33.

38. William W. Barton, "Respectability For Marketing," in *Marketing and Society: The Challenge*, ed. F. J. Lavidge and R. J. Holloway (Homewood, Ill.: Richard D. Irwin, 1969), p. 16.

39. Kotler and Zaltman, "Social Market," p. 7.

40. Ibid., p. 5.

41. L. T. Sargent, *Political Ideologies: A Comparative Analysis* (Homewood, Ill.: Dorsey Press, 1969), p. 69.

42. R. Y. Fluno, *The Democratic Community: Government Practices and Purposes* (New York: Dodd, Mead & Company, 1971), p. 7.

43. C. Cohen, *Democracy* (Athens: University of Georgia Press, 1971), p. 3.

44. Sargent, *Political Ideologies*, p. 87.

45. Fluno, *The Democratic Community*, p. 19.

46. M. Zimmerman, *Contemporary Problems of Democracy* (New York, Humanities Press, 1972), chap. 1.

47. Ibid., p. 31.

48. Thomas Jefferson, as quoted in G. H. Sabine and T. L. Thorson, *A History of Political Theory*, 4th ed. (Hinsdale, Ill.: Dryden Press, 1973), p. 608.

49. Zimmerman, *Contemporary Problems of Democracy*, p. 35.

50. Sargent, *Political Ideologies*, p. 29.

51. Great Britain, *Hansard's Parliamentary Debates* (Commons), 5th ser. 14 March 1977, p. 3967.

52. Fitness and Amateur Sport Directorate, "Special Report on Participaction," May 1977, p. 7.

53. F. Lowe, "Time for Little Guy to Start Complaining," *Fredericton* (New Brunswick) *Gleaner*, 29 December 1971.

54. Fluno, *The Democratic Community*, p. 9.

55. Zimmerman, *Contemporary Problems of Democracy*, p. 29.

56. R. N. Farmer, "Would You Want Your Daughter to Marry a Marketing Man?" in *Marketing and Society*, p. 11–15.

57. Kotler and Zaltman, "Social Marketing," p. 58.

The Development of Public Recreational Service Policy

Jay S. Shivers

People are interdependent creatures, and they live in a world that is totally related through interlocking ecological systems. Whatever a person does within his own habitat has significant and immediate effects on all other niches where life abounds. Sooner or later, the impact of population increments and the concomitant pollution, congestion, visual scarring, and displacement that unrestrained population growth brings must have a negative effect upon the biosphere and the supporting ecosystem. With rising affluence, mobility, and mass leisure, many national governments are beginning to appreciate the need for some form of planning that can regulate land use, conservation of natural resources, control of pollution, and development of priorities that can assure the greatest benefits to their constituencies.

Where governments have established the provision of recreational services, because they perceive it as a necessity in creating an environment that can enhance the human condition, public policy becomes the guidelines by which governmental jurisdiction fulfills this responsibility. As governments become more responsive to human needs, they will undertake those functions which provide for human betterment through ministries that offer both the instructional means and the protected natural resources capable of supplying the environment, leading to satisfaction through recreational experiences.

Any attempt at explaining the evolution of public policy as

Jay S. Shivers, Ph.D., is professor, Leisure and Recreation Studies, School of Education, University of Connecticut, Storrs, Connecticut, United States.

it pertains to recreational services must, therefore, be concerned with the intent of lawmakers. The authoritative source of responsibility lies with legislators understanding the need for public recreational services. Where legal or constitutional provisions of government decree the uplifting of human conditions and express a concern for the health, education, and welfare of the constituent population, there is the basis for the development of public recreational policy. Broadly speaking, constitutional references or legislation that upholds the concept of human rights must provide for people to exist in an environment that can support positive growth and development and not negate human progress. The human condition is closely associated with those experiences which promote basic satisfactions, encourage personal creativity, and heighten feelings of personal worth through self-expression and wholesome activities. Recreational experience may be one of the most beneficial sources for the free expression of personal satisfaction by self-actualization and self-realization. For that reason, government has come to see that recreational service is a responsibility of government at every level and as such requires both legislative mandate and financial support.

The twentieth century has seen the ongoing development of civilization devoting its energies to the mechanistic advances of science and technology. Technology has given rise to formidable production of consumer goods, defense capability, and transportation of goods and people on a scale heretofore unimaginable. Advances in medical science have enabled the gross environmental diseases to be all but obliterated, while nutritional science has done much to enhance the life cycle. Contemporary life moves to the tune of automated data processing, cybernetics, transitor cells, miniaturization, satellite communications, laser techniques, mass media, mass mobility, cheap money, mass education, and mass leisure—all expressive of a feverish eagerness for more abundant living.

The human horizon is infinitely enlarged, but the good life has somewhat deteriorated with urban conglomerations, congestion, oil shortages, power failures, mass unemployment, and lack of opportunity for life enrichment of those who have

not or cannot take advantage of either free public education or the environment for a higher quality of living. Scientific advancement is obvious, but the higher standard of living to which all look has not been sufficiently widespread to better humanity. The full educational and artistic aspects of living are still unrealized.

Although the United States offers tremendous individual opportunity, most people carry on a deadly routine and conformity in the midst of our vaunted individualism and freedom. There seems to be a tendency to follow the crowd, to dress as others dress, to read the same books, think the same thoughts, and march to the same drummer. Any attempt at variance is either tacitly disapproved or overtly chastised. Most people are afraid to be themselves if that means being different; there is fear about what others may say. Although secure in individual freedom and opportunity, we are insecure within ourselves as individuals; there is safety in conformity. Psychologically, many people are not mature.

Conformity has always been a part of the human community and is a definite characteristic of primitive and folk culture, of young life or adolescence, and of immature adult minds. It must be realized, however, that slavish conformity reflects a dominance of the acquisitiveness of human nature that takes over the creations of others without effort to know or understand. It is the easy way, but it is the attitude that quells the spirit of inquiry and the impulse to create. In consequence, rigid living patterns, distrust, and intolerance of others develop.

In order to assist in the maturation of people and to raise the cultural level, there must be provided the same opportunity for self-expression and cultural growth that has been afforded in those branches of learning which deal with the sciences. The humanities approach to education must, perforce, include all of the leisure arts. The creative, artistic, and other self-enhancing potentialities of people must be tapped and cultivated if the lives of people are to be enriched beyond mere materialism.

The development of such a program requires an under-

standing of the social, economic, political, and environmental conditions out of which a public policy can develop. Legislators and executives must recognize the problems of the times and discover answers that will offer commitment and provide the resources necessary to fulfill the needs of contemporary life. Policy cannot express feelings and ideals that have long since vanished or adopt techniques and aims without consideration of their pertinence. The problems of contemporary society must be born in mind, and solutions through recreational services must be found.

In a pluralistic society with a republic form of government based upon capitalistic economics, the idea of any governmental agency at any level attempting to manage the leisure of people is abhorrent. The people's leisure, whatever it is, is wholly their own. They have complete discretion as to what they will do with such free time, how they will perform, and where and when they will undertake activity or do nothing. Of course, it must be understood that leisure use is predicated upon responsible behavior that is socially acceptable. It is not meant that individuals may give way to anarchical activity that infringes upon the rights of others or act in ways that are reprehensible, illegal, or immoral. There are people who use their leisure in antisocial ways. They perform delinquent acts and demean themselves in the process. But these individuals are subject to the criminal justice system and would behave in pathological ways whether they have leisure or not.

This discussion is concerned with the ways in which government, through its policy, attempts to manipulate or direct citizens in their use of leisure. Despite the best intentions, insofar as cultural enhancement, physical fitness, skill development, self-expression, or self-actualization is concerned, government can provide opportunities but cannot require participation. It may be true that most people do not know what is best for them in terms of healthful living, appreciation of the arts, knowledge of current events, or participation in the political process that affects them, but it is intolerable for any government to try to dictate how people will utilize their leisure—except that it may not be used illegally.

Through the provision of public recreational service and the endowment of the performing arts in all of their manifestations, government can provide the setting and the opportunity so that people may choose from among several alternatives how they wish to spend their leisure. To the extent that government has been lax or negligent about its sponsorship of the arts (and by extension, the field of public recreational service), opportunities for making choices dwindle. However, government at all levels recognizes the importance of recreational activity in the lives of citizens and has therefore developed agencies that can render recreational services. This has come about through the conscious development of public policy pertinent to the conservation of natural resources; the provision of facilities, supplies, and leadership necessary for the instruction and guidance of potential recreational clientele; and the funding of such organizations designed to bring a higher quality of life to those who must rely solely upon the public sector for their recreational opportunities. Though all of this is valid, there should never be formalized policy wherein the government attempts to achieve political consensus or to press some ideological view through the manner in which it supports recreational service or the way in which it attempts to channel people's behavior during leisure.

Out of the change and advocacy for better services must also come the realization that the field of recreational service is not a leisure management enterprise. At best, recreationists may manage facilities, areas, supplies, equipment, personnel, and finances to best perform those services which guarantee recreational opportunities. However, the recreationist is a resource, not a director; a guide, not a dictator; a leader, not a magistrate; an educator, not a warden. Recreational service is a permissive rather than mandatory function. People do not have to participate in the activities that the public agency offers. Participation is absolutely voluntary and valued only to the extent that the individual achieves whatever goal he sets for himself, whether it be an instructional, skill, entertainment, or enjoyment objective. Of course, it might very well be a combination of all of these. Nevertheless, the essential

objective of the field of recreational service is to offer a variety of recreational opportunities in which people may engage. The offerings may be of any kind as long as they are ethically derived. As professionals, recreationists are obliged to enhance human efforts and not to practice in any way that would demean their constituencies, the field, or themselves.

In the next few years, recreationists will be called upon to exercise greater concern for a larger number of people than they have before, but they will not manage people's leisure. To manage really means to control or to render submissive. Recreationists do not control leisure, nor is the public submissive to the importunings of the field in the guise of its various agencies. Our social role is the husbanding of natural resources for public use—the coordination of men, materials, and money in a way that provides recreational opportunity to whoever wishes to undertake such opportunities. If the field fulfills its role, then recreationists will be acting in advisory and advocacy capacities. Recreationists must always be mindful that they are servants, not masters. In the public sector of society, the recreationist ministers to the needs of people insofar as he is permitted by those people to counsel or instruct them.

Documentation of public recreational policy by reference to philosophical statements contained within the various constitutions, codes, and statutes of any state indicates the best available definitions of what it is that public agencies and their ministerial officers may do. Among legislative accords would be those which have important contributions for the support of public recreational service. These may be illustrated through the following examples:

1. The authorization of governments to establish systems of playgrounds, public parks, libraries, and other institutions and to perform services for the purpose of providing recreational experiences for all the people
2. The establishment of standards that are concerned with the preparation and selection of qualified professional personnel to administer and to supply leadership for recreational service

3. The fostering by the government of the preparation of children and youth for the wholesome use of leisure
4. The enactment of legislation to protect, conserve, and develop the natural resources and wildlife of the jurisdiction; to preserve the rights of the people to the coast and to coastal waterways, if any; or to conserve inland waterways against encroachment and pollution—all of which are useful for recreational purposes
5. The opening of public buildings and grounds as centers where groups of citizens may meet for informal recreation activities
6. The authorization of the expenditure of funds for acquisition and improvement of land and water areas for parks and other recreational purposes
7. The organization of government agencies to plan for, coordinate, and provide such recreational resources as forests, beaches, historical monuments, empounded water areas for recreational use and wildlife conservation and to develop institutes, workshops, or conferences for the administration of leadership and program courses.

Public policy does not, however, evolve from nothing. There must be substantial groundwork developed by community leaders and interested spokesmen who have the capacity to educate and to disseminate their views on the need for the public recreational service administration. When there is an insistent public clamor for governmental initiation of programs that can effectively deal with recreational provisions, some public policy will be forthcoming. Citizen demand slowly builds as interest, knowledge, and capacity to perform materializes. As citizens reach a state of awareness about deficits that they perceive government can alleviate, there is a vociferous demand for governmental intervention. It is at this point that policy becomes articulated and translated into substantive activities carried out by ministerial departments. Education is the primary requisite for the institution of public policy; it is a slow, painful, but necessary procedure if sufficient pressure is to be exerted upon those legislators who will ultimately fashion public policy from insistent constituent request.

Governmental policy for recreational services must be based on the needs of the people. The entire foundation of public recreational service should be a reflection of diverse needs, interests, abilities, and values, as well as common points of interest. Opportunities for participation should be available to all of the people insofar as it is possible for publicly administered agencies to serve the multifarious needs, interests, and demands of a heterogeneous population. In any case, there should be a basic program of recreational opportunities available that offers satisfaction of the major recreational desires that citizens seek within the context of the community. Cooperative efforts will assure additional opportunity with additional cost.

Recreational planning is one element on which public policy is based. It is concerned with, among other things, developing recreational places through which the communitywide program can effectively accommodate participants. It is also involved in the distribution of recreational spaces and physical facilities throughout the entire community. The allocation of various types of spaces and facilities is based upon present demographic analysis as well as projection of population density, movement, characteristics, and other elements that indicate where specific recreational sites should be situated for present and future utilization. There should be no such concept as equitable distribution of recreational places. Placement of facilities and areas should be predicated on present and future needs. Neither urban ghetto slums nor "gold coast" neighborhoods should receive or be deprived of facilities and spaces because of what or who they represent. Need is the single criterion on which recreational places should be distributed, developed, and programmed.

Land spaces and structures, together with their planned allocation, are the foundations for a system of public recreational service. These places provide the environment in which the citizens' use of leisure may seek expression and fruition. A system of recreational places include a wide variety of areas and structures, including playgrounds, playfields, parks, reservations, arboretums, botanical and zoological gardens, golf links, beaches, swimming pools, auditoriums, gymnasiums, shelters, band shells, and a host of other facilities. Because these places must be designed to satisfy the present and developing organized recreational program and the self-directed activities engaged in by citizens of the community, the recreationist has to recognize certain fundamental premises on which any public service is based. Thus, public policy is mindful of the following factors:

1. Places in which self-directed activities can occur should be provided. Such facilities and areas would be operated without direct leadership or organized activities. Protective and custodial personnel may be required, and the facility would probably be managed under a formal set of rules and regulations or by some licensing procedure.
2. Recreational places that are appropriate for highly organized and guided experiences under the direct supervision of recreationists should be provided.
3. The economic base of the community, and by wider implication, the state and nation, is a vital factor. All of the economically directed activities that produce wealth and upon which the financial well-being of the population is based tend to influence the financial support that recreational services receive. The development of the physical plant to best serve the recreational needs of citizens rests predominantly upon financial support and the commitment of the population to the acquisition, development, and operation of places for recreational activities. Unless the community is willing to provide the financial assistance necessary for the expense of planning and development, little can be done that will have a salutary effect upon the recreational enrichment of the lives of the citizens. Financial considerations, which include the tax base and rates, property values, outstanding bond issues, limitations on community indebtedness, community revenues, and the probability of the local governments' sustaining capital expenditures over a generation for the comprehensive physical recreational plan are also involved.

4. The nature and philosophy of governmental jurisdictions should also be carefully investigated. Political concepts and the effects of pressure groups stimulating changing values and responsibilities of local governing bodies will have a marked effect on public policy. Reactionary forces invariably contemplate reduced governmental spending for such functions as recreational service. They seek retrenchment and a return to less governmental involvement in the lives of people. This necessarily reveals itself in fewer services of various kinds, a reversion to status quo interests, and an attempt to impede promotional programs and to favor more a restrictive climate. Libertarian forces, on the other hand, are almost diametrically opposed to any restriction on human development. The possibility of planning for public recreational services would be vastly different given either of these types of governmental policy. What is valid for the extremes of government is also true for the several positions that the party in power might take on any number of issues presented to it. It is not surprising, therefore, that any planning capability by recreational service agencies would necessarily reflect the political philosophy of the governing faction as well as influences brought to bear upon the political system by vocal minorities, the moderate majority, and outside social, political, or economic impingements that might have a telling effect upon the jurisdiction's institutions and policies.

5. Great effort must be made to educate the constituency to the needs and values that will provide direct benefit to them. The public should be kept constantly in mind because it is by public opinion that support for public recreational service is developed and maintained. Unless the policymakers recognize popular demand, there is always the possibility of inaction or of rejection of proposals that appear too progressive or too conducive to rapid change. Programming is facilitated when popular support is aroused in its favor. Such support is stimulated through good public relations, education, and a systematic appeal to reason.

6. Every effort to coordinate the resources and expertise of

the various sectors of society should be acted upon. Public, quasi-public, and private agencies have complementary functions that can be useful to the greater community when properly coordinated.

7. The value of existing national and state agencies whose orientation may be inclined toward recreational service directly or secondarily should be recognized and utilized in the planning process. Such agencies have some responsibility and may be capable of beneficial contributions to the overall process.

Of course, public policy may also be generated by far-sighted legislators and ministerial executives who realize the need for policy long before public consumption brings public awakening. They will not only write the policy necessary for the encouragement of governmental recreational service, but will also lead the public toward a recognition of their own needs and the benefits to be derived from such governmental action.

The creation and implementation of public policy must be concerned with equality of opportunity. Every person has the innate right to pursue his dreams and must be given the opportunity to fulfill his needs, within the bounds of societal approval and within his capacity, without artificial hindrance. The standard upon which policy should be determined is whether each individual has had an opportunity to take advantage of activities offered, not whether he has actually participated. There should be no stipulation as to the amount of service received. In fact, equality of service is neither possible nor practical because of great individual differences. To the extent that some people need a good deal more attention than others (in terms of instructional assistance, personal guidance, activity direction, or other supervision), there will always be a disproportionate amount of service administered. This will occur because of the very nature of recreational services: there are too many people in comparison to the number of professional personnel employed within the field, and there is no way that every person can be reached.

Every person must be given his share, his opportunity to

perform. Whether one utilizes this opportunity is incidental; the *chance* to participate is paramount. Insofar as this opportunity is one of recreational experience, it is limited to those satisfactions which may be gained through activities in a recreational context. But beyond offering the opportunity to participate or not to participate, recreationists have the professional obligation of providing stimulating activities involving all phases of human life. There must be something for everybody. Activities should range as wide as the human mind is capable of expanding, with emphasis upon those events which tend to enlighten through social, cultural, and educational experiences.

Even when progress is made in the issuance of public policy, it remains for implementation to carry out legislative intent. Policymakers cannot be oblivious of the future, which imposes responsibilities to be confronted. That which seemed reasonably adequate in the past will be insufficient for the future. Everything essential to wholesome living will be required in greater quantity and higher quality. There are several reasons for this:

1. The population continues to increase.
2. Time available for recreation will continue to increase at an even faster pace than formerly.
3. Open land suitable for recreational purposes and essential to the preservation of the natural landscape is being occupied, rendering it increasingly difficult to provide appropriate sites for leisure activities.
4. Increased discretionary income, mobility, and leisure time constitute a reservoir of demand that will alert citizens to their own needs and make them importunate in their claims and generous in their support of well-developed plans to meet those needs.

Policy is the guide by which legislators and ministerial agents can initiate programs and structures. By making decisions enabling each citizen to seek opportunities for cultural development in the broadest sense, policymakers at all governmental levels will insure the continuing capacity of public agencies to perform in ways that are beneficial to the constituency. When functionaries formulate policy, it is vital that openness, leadership, integrity, and competence are promoted. These are the bases for an enlightened public policy dealing with the recreational use of leisure.

The Urban Framework for Leisure: Implications for Community Living

Livin Bollaert

Urbanization is a universal process. Each year, thousands of houses are built in the industrialized countries; it is estimated that by the year 2000, over half of the world's population will live in urban areas. Urbanization, at least as far as Belgium and most West European countries are concerned, does not only involve the extension of existing cities, but also affects the villages. The prospect of progressing urbanization may be rather unappealing to many, but it is nevertheless an irreversible process.

The question, therefore, is not so much whether the increase of urbanization on a large scale is to be considered as progress or regression, but how we will manage to live with this frightening reality in the future.

Living in the city is becoming ever more disagreeable, for such reasons as crowding, noise, smell, and alienation. In a city, people live closer to each other but have less contact than in other areas. Neighbors may not even know each other. It is impossible, of course, to give a full account of all the problems of living in the city. I shall therefore, as was required, confine myself to one of the problems—namely, the problem of leisure and recreation in urbanized areas.

We accept the idea that just as the working environment affects one's work life, the residential milieu strongly influences life outside the work place. The term *residential*, or

Livin Bollaert, Ph.D., is professor and chairman, Department of Physical Education and Recreation, the Free University of Brussels, Belgium.

116

living environment involves the style of living and housing, in all its social and environmental aspects. A very important reason that leisure and recreation in the city may be a problem lies in the actual concepts of housing and the residential environment.

Builders, promoters, and authorities consider the house to be a very profitable article of mass production, and this attitude brings housing and the residential environment into the financial and economic sector. The building of housing developments is a business where profit comes first; and as is often the case when profit is the rule, certain sometimes vital interests are put aside or simply ignored. It is clear that these interests are the quality of life in general and the quality of housing and living in particular. The fact that residential environment is concerned with a market product in very high demand (namely, housing in or near the city) is not likely to make things easier. Because of the actual scarcity of houses, there is little chance of finding available housing except at relatively high cost. As a result, developers and promotors will sacrifice quality for quantity.

The attitude of the authorities toward housing is not very different. The postwar housing policy was dominated by the question of how to house the maximum number of families at minimum costs. I must also point to the fact that city authorities would in most cases (for purely financial reasons) prefer to sell expensive city land to the highest bidders among building firms rather than to reserve them for non- or low-profit recreation units, parks, or public housing projects. I could refer to many scandals of land speculation that seem to have become almost classic, but this is probably not the place or time to go into details.

If the authorities show some willingness to change the residential environment in a positive way, in most cases it is done in what can be labeled as a quantitative-technical approach. An example of this approach is the standard by which for each inhabitant X square meters of open space must be allotted in a given housing area, or by which there must be a swimming pool of X cubic meters per 1,000 inhabitants. Quality, organization, and design are not taken into account.

An example typical of such an approach has been discovered in the course of leisure research that is being carried out by my department of the Free University of Brussels—research that aims at measuring the factors that influence the participation in sports and cultural activities of the population of Brussels. This specific case concerned a socially deprived neighborhood in Brussels, inhabited mainly by older people and immigrants. Social workers working in that area had been asking the local authorities for small, scattered playfields.

It can not be said for certain whether the expensive, large and prestigious sports center built afterward was the result of this plea; anyway, the local population makes little or no use of it. A survey showed that the local population wanted small playfields or courts that anybody could use at any time. The only equipment asked for was basketball baskets. The sophisticated sports center, where mainly organized sports are practiced and available courts must be rented, clearly does not answer the needs of a broad segment of the local population.

This example shows that the quantitative-technical approach in the field of urbanization is a derogation of the opportunity of individual self-expression. The inhabitants stand little chance of having their demands concerning the quality of their environment realized. The responsibility for this may be attributed mainly to the fact that—certainly in larger cities—experts (public or private) are in charge of designing and planning the residential environment, and the inhabitants must try to live with their frustrations.

Only on very rare occasions can people identify with their environment. By *identification* I mean the act of possession, being able and allowed to change a house in one's own way to meet one's own wishes and needs. This identification can only be complete if the inhabitants have the opportunity to put something of themselves into their environment, in their own houses as well as in their neighborhood. It is therefore supposed that the house as well as the neighborhood should have a certain built-in flexibility, so that alterations of houses and neighborhoods are possible if the necessity presents itself. A maximum freedom in living and housing should be aimed at.

This freedom, which is indispensable for the individual's identification with his residential milieu, is not available in most cases. In many cases, further restrictions are imposed. For example, in many public housing developments in Belgium, keeping and raising chickens, rabbits, or other pets in the yard is not allowed. Sometimes it is also forbidden to plant gardens in the front yards—the pretext being that the uniformity of the neighborhood must be preserved. In the Foyer-Bruxellois-Brusselse Haard (a neighborhood of public housing), it is formally forbidden to put posters up in the windows. In certain neighborhoods in the Netherlands, regulations go so far as demanding that people hang the same curtains.

It is obvious that in this age, which is already characterized by a high degree of alienation on all levels, such restrictive rules make identification with one's environment very difficult, if not impossible. Eventually identification boils down to the desire to situate oneself in society as a whole.

Public housing still bears too much of the mark of being a favor, as though the inhabitant ought to be thankful to the politician, the owner, or the promoter for being allowed to live there. In the present situation of scarcity, the inhabitant will often be obliged to make allowances in his way of life, and the owner will be inclined to impose restrictions on the tenants. The architects, owners, promoters, and politicians should consider the wishes and needs of the inhabitants when making decisions, because they are the ones who are going to have to live in the houses. It is, however, not that simple. There is, for instance, the problem of gathering information and the question of how to bridge the gap between owners, architects, and policymakers on the one hand and the inhabitants on the other, in order to get to know the latter's needs.

Scientific research will have to contribute largely to solving these problems and should not be confined to a mere gathering of wishes concerning housing. Scientific research must interpret these wishes in relation to other elements of behavior and place them within the actual situation (work, finances, social conditions, etc.) of the inhabitants. It is clear that it will be possible to apply the results of scientific research only if the owners and planners show the will to solve the housing problem.

It should be evident by now that the way of living, the housing situation, and the residential milieu will strongly affect the recreation patterns of the urban population. Before going into these recreation patterns, however, I would like to describe first what I mean by *recreation*.

In our society, leisure time and work time are strictly separated. In this view of leisure, which is adopted by many social and political scientists, leisure time is the time that is used to compensate for strains resulting from monotonous or stressful work. Leisure (or recreation) is therefore only a compensation—a kind of bed to rest in after a hard day's work in order to go back refreshed and brisk the next day. This means that recreation and leisure are seen only in terms of work. This bourgeois concept of leisure and recreation is a direct result, even an extension, of the existing relationships within production whereby the worker, obliged to sell his labor, becomes totally alienated from both his work and the product of his work, in which he is denied—and this is very important—any form of creativity or personal involvement. At the same time, recreation and leisure are seen as an autonomous part of life, being dependent upon the labor process, but separate from it.

In my view, however, this vision profoundly underestimates recreation. I am convinced that recreation involves a form of self-realization, whereby the individual tries to become integrated into his environment, his neighborhood, and his society as a whole. Recreation and leisure activities should therefore aim at integration in society. When talking about integration, it must be clearly stated that this word refers to one's total life in society, which cannot be separated into spheres of work, recreation, and so on.

This brings us back to the theme of housing and the residential environment. *Residential environment* does not refer simply to a collection of houses protecting people against cold and rain. The street must be given other functions than accommodating traffic; for instance, walking, meeting, and playing. Pedestrian malls are rare in Belgium, unlike in some other

West European countries (such as the Netherlands), and in most cases they have only one function: to facilitate shopping.

Apparently the main problem of the residential environment is that its functions are being curtailed, mostly because of motives involving economic imperatives (fast traffic, shopping centers), while the environment of recreation is being ignored. It is not unusual, for example, for children to walk several kilometers to find a playground, because there is none in their own neighborhood. During weekends, inhabitants of Brussels will drive twenty, thirty, and up to a hundred kilometers to enjoy nature in a provincial recreation park.

Life has become compartmentalized. There is the shopping center if one wants to go shopping; there is the sports center to practice sports; there are specific areas for working and marked paths for walking. Likewise the street, once the stage for all social life, now belongs entirely to the car.

The housing developments currently being planned and built are generally failing to meet requirements of integration and multiple function. Even where there is enough space, many facilities that are in great demand are not offered, while the existing facilities show so little design and organization that they can only partially reach their goals. As the situation now stands, all age and activity groups are lacking the opportunities to participate in recreational activities in their own neighborhoods. This especially affects the groups with strong ties to the neighborhood; for instance, children, older people, housewives, and the handicapped.

To illustrate this I refer again to the example of the deprived area in Brussels. The younger population of that neighborhood had been asking for a few open-air basketball courts. The older people, a primarily native and less mobile population group, had asked to have benches placed around these basketball courts. The intention was clear: they wanted the opportunity to meet people of their own age in their own neighborhood and at the same time have the opportunity to watch the younger people playing. It is highly unlikely that any of these people had ever read any literature concerning social integration. I believe that this example clearly shows that social integration is not simply a theoretic concoction by a few highly specialized social scientists; on the contrary, it is a reflection of real and fundamental needs.

The activities of one person may lead to passive involvement of another—a process that also occurs in fields other than recreation. In this respect, the neighborhood should offer a number of opportunities to make informal contacts, both between people of the same generation and people of several generations.

As antipode of multiple-function, the functional differentiation characterizing present residential milieu especially in the cities—(which in fact, is a direct result of the social and economic context) forms the strongest obstruction for integration. In the future this fact must be taken into account, certainly when developing research on the recreation needs of people in their own surroundings.

In the past, housing research has focused on the house and has shown little interest in the total environment. Such research will meet with success only if it aims at integration. If the experts are to make the decisions, they will have to base them on the results of a thorough consultation with the population groups involved. It may be interesting to give a short account of how *participation* was defined for interdisciplinary research work on the participation of the population of Brussels in sports and cultural activities. Starting with the idea of integration, *participation* was defined as a regular, active, or passive participation—individually or in groups—in activities or happenings taking place during free time, which are to a greater or lesser degree aimed at a varied public, and which create an opportunity for social interaction. The last element (namely, the opportunity for social interaction) was considered to be an especially important part of integration. And it is precisely this integration, when realized on all levels and in all areas of social life (including housing) that will be the solution to widespread and destructive alienation and the means to attractive recreation and leisure programming in urban areas.

The Disabled and the Community: Establishing Humanistic Recreation and Leisure Policies for the Future

Joseph Levy

Ladies and gentlemen, it is only fitting that this international seminar on molding leisure policies for educational, communal, and labor frameworks include in its agenda a session on the disabled. The organizers of this conference are to be commended for their sensitivity and foresight as scientists and human beings.

The famous seventeenth-century English poet, John Donne (1572–1631), said, "No man is an island, entire of itself; every man is a piece of the continent, a part of the main."

We as leisure and recreation professionals and scientists living on the frontier of the twenty-first century are part of an exciting and dynamic era in the delivery of human services. It is my belief that the 1970s, 1980s, and 1990s will someday be referred to in the historical archives as consciousness-raising decades on behalf of the minorities and disabled in our communities.

Never before in the recorded history of the civilized world have we witnessed such global concern, tolerance, acceptance, and accommodation for the rights and needs of minority groups, ethnic groups, women, children, homosexuals, the aged, and those afflicted with mental, physical, and social disabilities. To me, these trends pose a vast and exciting challenge to those of us who want to provide more humanistic and

Joseph Levy, Ph.D., is associate professor, Department of Recreation, University of Waterloo. He is also the director of the Sport and Leisure Resource Centre for Special Populations, University of Waterloo, Waterloo, Ontario, Canada.

growth-producing leisure and recreation experience for all our citizens. Any sound formulation of professional policies for the future requires the establishment of an ideology or philosophy of human services. For without some consensus on this ideology or philosophy, our policies lack any meaningful raison d'être. I should now like to outline the major philosophical hallmarks of recreation and leisure services for the disabled and then follow these axioms with some specific policy suggestions.

Philosophical Premises for the Delivery of Recreation and Leisure Services for the Disabled

Disability vs. Handicap
The first humanistic principle that has to surface is the need to distinguish, semantically and operationally, between the usage of the words *disability* and *handicap*.

Is a disabled person one who is unable to do anything? This, of course, is an absurdity that calls forth the rebuttal that the designation is meant to refer to varying degrees of disability and not just to the extreme. More accurately, then, a physically disabled person is also a physically abled person. There are things that he can do as well as things that he cannot do. We may conclude that the designation, a *physically disabled person*, is a shortcut to the more involved but psychosocially sounder expression, a *person with a physical disability*. Such a reformulation has far-reaching humanistic implications for leisure service planners, for it suggests that a person with a disability is first a person, with many unique and creative characteristics in addition to a particular disability. I am sure that some of you will have the feeling that this is much ado about nothing, but I can assure you that it is precisely this conception of a person with a physical disability as a physically disabled person that has reduced all his spheres of interaction to the disability aspects of his physique—leisure services included.

While I cannot speak for all of the nations represented here today, I can authoritatively state that it was not until 1975 that a person with a physical disability was accepted into a medical program at a Canadian University.

We may now ask wherein lies the distinction between the so-called disabled and normal, since omnipotence is not a property of any mortal creature on earth, and all of us must function within more or less defined limits. Only three years ago we witnessed Lasse Viren, the Finnish long-distance runner, win two gold medals at the Montreal Olympic Games. It is a medical fact that Viren suffers from a blood disorder that necessitates specific treatment and diet. Lasse Viren's case demonstrates the fact that the concept of disability implies, not inability, but a deviation from a normal standard, deviation from a state that is natural or average.

It would be a travesty and injustice to the majority of the Israeli people to suggest that they consider themselves handicapped because cannot run so fast as Finland's Lasse Viren, jump so high as Canada's Greg Joy, or be so strong and agile as decathlon gold medalist Bruce Jenner of the United States.

I would now like to propose a distinction between the terms *disability* and *handicap* that should become an integral, humanistic component of your leisure policy planning process. A disability is an objective condition of impairment—physical, mental, social, or emotional—that can usually be described by a professionally trained individual such as a physician, psychologist, educator, or social worker. A handicap is the cumulative result of the physical, social, vocational, educational, and other obstacles that the disability interposes between the individual and his optimal functional level. A disability, then, is more particularly an objective deviation from the norm, whereas a handicap more nearly refers to the secondary normative barriers imposed upon the disabled individual. Thus we may say that the handicapped person is a person who, because of his physical, social, intellectual, or emotional disabilities, cannot or is not permitted by the non-disabled members of society to function in his various parental, vocational, civic, and leisure roles. And hence we may see that the converse follows: If the individual with a physical, social, intellectual, or emotional disability were socialized to function optimally in society in his various roles, then he would not be handicapped.

In short, policy planners of humanistic leisure service systems must not contribute toward forcing people with disabilities to become handicapped.

Normalization Principle

The second humanistic principle that is offered as a policy planning guide for leisure services with the disabled comes to us from the Scandinavian countries.[1] For decades, the principle of normalization has guided the planning of human services for the disabled in the Scandinavian countries. The normalization principle means making available to the disabled patterns and conditions of everyday life that are as close as possible to the norms and patterns of the mainstream of society. The normalization principle implies a normal rhythm of life—a rhythm of family life, working, playing, growing, traveling, visiting, and so on.

An essential part of the principle of normalization is the concept of integration. The last decade has witnessed great process toward ending the segregation of the disabled from life around them. Many who in the past would have been allowed to vegetate in cribs, wheelchairs, backrooms, and overcrowded institutions are being integrated into the normal rhythm of community life. It is only the most severely disabled who require institutionalization.

The normalization principle is as yet far from an accepted norm in my Canadian society. People are still very reluctant to work, live, or play next to a paraplegic, diabetic, mongoloid, amputee, or emotionally disturbed adolescent. Most Canadians would prefer to see the disabled segregated from the nondisabled when it comes to sharing human services. This fact has been supported by research carried out in the United States and Canada.

Two years ago, a group of my students carried out a winter sports and recreation program for mentally retarded adults living in a segregated residence five miles outside of a rural hamlet. The winter program was implemented at a community skiing facility. It was evident from the passive and active resistance experienced by the student organizers and the mentally retarded participants that the members of this community leisure center were not in favor of facilitating the integration of a group of mongoloid adults into their leisure and personal space. There was concern expressed by some of the more active and vocal members of the skiing club that some of the friendly mongols may be potentially dangerous, and they thought that their children should not be exposed to people who lived in institutions.

This case clearly points out the self-fulfilling prophecy of our segregation policies in offering services to the disabled. We force and shape these people to behave and respond as we think that they should—we keep the retarded, retarded; we keep the physically disabled immobile and isolated; we keep the emotionally insecure, insecure; we keep the supposedly senile, senile; and so on down the line of disabilities.

Some individuals deny that persons with disabilities are deprived of normalizing experiences. They argue that we have some of the finest "Special Olympics" and "crippled" programs. I would concur with that viewpoint 100 percent. Suffice it to say, however, that the concept of normalization is the antithesis of offering Special Olympics and crippled programs. We must put an end to the patronizing, stigmatizing attitude of our society that fosters an inferior and special status for the disabled. Segregated community leisure services *for* the disabled must become integrated community leisure services *with* the disabled.

Every member of our community will grow and learn to appreciate his own unique abilities and disabilities through the integration of all differentially endowed citizens. Based upon my own personal experience and the research studies carried out in such countries as Israel, Denmark, and Holland, it may be unequivocally stated that nondisabled children who are socialized to accept and live with various disabled groups grow up to be more compassionate, more humble, more perceptive, and more humane.

Human Leisure Services within a Humane Framework

The third and last humanistic principle that I should like to share with you today is based on a personal belief and professional commitment that all human leisure services can and must be planned within a humane framework.

The primordal goal of any of our leisure services—be they arts, sports, parks, zoos, scouts, guides, or what have you— *must be to promote and maintain the dignity and value of the individual.* We are indeed our brothers' keepers when we design our facilities and programs to permit the participation of all our citizens. Our philosophies must change so that our future planning reflects the ultimate concern for the equitable and optimal delivery of leisure services to those who are not so fast, strong, smart, secure, agile, or rich as the majority of society.

In short, those of our leisure servies which fail to accept responsibility for all of society's weaker and more dependent members are not operating with a humanistic framework.

Policies for Future Recreation and Leisure Services and the Disabled

What are some specific policies that should be foremost in our recreation and leisure planning for the disabled?

Labeling and Classification of Disabilities

First, all labeling and classifying of disabilities need to be seriously examined and minimized in all circumstances. Recreation and leisure professionals and scientists need to study the advantages and disadvantages of stereotyping people in terms of their disabilities. Recent clinical evidence would seem to indicate that labeling fosters the development of recreation and leisure services to suit the *anticipated* medical and clinical diagnosis of the individual. The last thing in the world that we want recreation and leisure services to become is self-fulfilling illness models.[2]

Therapy-Recreation Continuum

Historically, recreation and leisure services for the disabled were conceived and implemented within a "therapeutic" or "adapted" clinical model. Both these models were based on

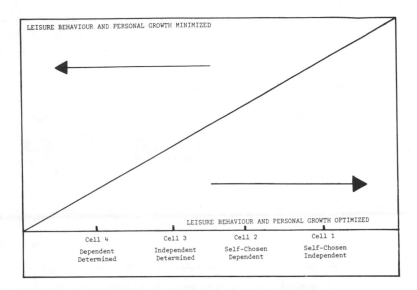

FIG. 1. RELATIONSHIP BETWEEN VOLITION AND REHABILITATION

the assumption that recreation and leisure programs for the disabled had to result in a therapeutic goal and consequently had to be subjected to all the adaptations and dicta necessary to bring about a prescribed change in the client. I and others have argued that these medical models of creation and leisure services may be used as rationales for supporting segregated and dependent roles at the sacrifice of encouraging more independent and growth-producing integrated programs and services.[3]

Presented in Figure 1 and Figure 2 is the relationship between client volition and rehabilitation goals. From these models, it is possible to see that many of our recreation and leisure services for the disabled are still operating in Cell 4. We need to stimulate normative policies that would aim for recreation and leisure services in Cells 1 and 2. We must begin to examine those of our recreation and leisure policies which segregate and devalue people because of their social, emotional, physical, or economic traits. To begin with, a serious examination of the value and role of "elite" sporting events for

VOLITION DIMENSION		
	Self-Chosen	Determined
Independent	**1** ●Recreation and leisure an end in itself ●Activity chosen for its own sake - not therapeutically oriented ●Intrinsically motivated ● e.g.: Lifting weights at the YMHA with the "weight lifting club".	**3** ●Choice of activity dictated by bio-physio-socio factors of the individual and environment ●Blind individual chooses to lift weights in his basement since he has no access to public facilities.
Dependent	**2** ●Recreation and leisure self-chosen, yet congruent with overall rehabilitation needs ●Intrinsically and extrinsically motivated ●e.g.: Lifting weights at the YMHA with the "weight lifting club", to improve respiratory capacity.	**4** ●"Therapeutic" and "Adapted" ●Concommitant of individual "therapeutic" needs and bio-physio-socio factors of the individual and environment ●Incarcerated young person who needs to acquire social skills that are not deviant is constricted to "socialize" only within the institution.

REHABILITA-
TION
DIMENSION

FIG. 2. DIMENSIONS OF VOLITION AND REHABILITATION

the disabled is suggested. Some have argued that these sporting extravaganzas are a camouflage and a deterrent from more fundamental issues and concerns.[4]

Professional-Consumer Relationships

There presently exists a movement in our society toward demystifying professional roles. Lawyers, doctors, teachers, and other professionals are being challenged by consumers at all levels. The basic concerns expressed by a literate and informed consumer are, "To what extent can we trust professionals to solve our serious personal and community problems?" and "Will people and communities grow more if they attempt to solve their own problems?"[5]

As recreation and leisure services move away from Cell 4 and into Cell 1, there will develop a decline of reliance on professionals for direct service. It is thus anticipated that many groups of disabled people will in the future require professionals simply to act as facilitators or catalysts as opposed to performers of direct service roles. Policies generated to encourage less reliance on direct professional expertise and more reliance on the skills and resources of the disabled will lead to three positive results:

1) A more respectful and honest relationship will develop between the consumer of the service and the provider of the service. The disabled will begin to feel as though their ideas and skills are worthwhile and can be used to contribute toward their own needs. This will eliminate the extreme-dependence model that has operated to date.
2) A thorough review of all recreation and leisure services will take place with the aim of assessing these services from the client's viewpoint rather than the traditional professional viewpoint.
3) Perhaps most important, the disabled will feel that they are no different than all the other citizens in the community who exercise the same right to determine the quality and quantity of their services. In the past, the disabled have been extremely reluctant to express any

SERVICE ROLE	LEADER COMPETENCIES	ADVANTAGES	DISADVANTAGES
DIRECT PROVIDER (Manufacturer - Consumer Roles)	•Programme planning/implementation •Growth and development needs	•Programme is pre-assembled •Easiest and most efficient method	•Client picks and chooses in "cafeteria" style •Programme prescribed by staff •Minimum input from clients •Facility centered approach requires clients to find and use programmes
FACILITATOR ROLE	•Facilitating or enabling •Coordination and referral •Work with many disciplines and services	•Synergetic programming •Financial cooperation •Information exchange •Client served by host of agencies	•Good cooperation required •Inventory of existing agencies •Client needs to develop understanding of system •Hard-to-reach missed
OUTREACH ROLE	•Community development skills •Personal rapport and communication •Understanding of barriers to participation	•Hard-to-reach clients contacted-missionary role •Work with all client groups •Programmes brought to clients who cannot attend programmes at Centres	•Time consuming •Supervision difficult •Dangerous •Community acceptance

FIG. 3. LEISURE AND RECREATION SERVICE DELIVERY ROLES TO OPTIMIZE CLIENT OPPORTUNITIES

disenchantment with their services for fear of insulting the providers of professional services.

Service Delivery Roles for a Pluralistic Community

Recognition of the pluralistic nature of the disabled members of our community lies at the heart of developing an optimum program delivery strategy for recreation and leisure services. The need to adopt differential approaches to programming in order to effectively accommodate the variety of needs and interests held by diverse disabled client groups is a primary challenge facing future recreation and leisure service systems.

The disabled community is far from being a homogeneous population; in fact, they are as heterogeneous a mix of subpopulations as one would find among the nondisabled. The disabled can thus be differentiated along age, income, background, and motivation lines just like all other client groups in the community. Recognition of the pluralistic nature of the disabled client group lies at the heart of formulating policies for the optimal delivery of recreation and leisure services. Policies will have to be developed around three primary delivery roles: (1) the direct provider role, (2) the facilitator role, and (3) the outreach role.[6] Presented in Figure 3 are the three service delivery roles that will have to be developed to serve the heterogeneous disabled clientele.

Since this whole paper was based on the premise that sometime down the road all recreation and leisure services will cater to all the citizens of the community, I challenge all of you today to design and recommend policies that will minimize handicaps, eliminate segregation, and foster the dignity and creativity of the individual regardless of his unique characteristics and needs.

NOTES

1. W. Wolfensberger, *The Principle of Normalization in Human Services* (Toronto: National Institute on Mental Retardation, 1972).

2. I. Illich et al., *Disabling Professions* (London: Marion Boyars, 1977); J. Lord,

"New Directions and New Roles: A View of Physical Activity and Disabled Individuals for the 1990s" (paper delivered at the Canadian Council of University Physical Education Administrators, Brock University, Saint Catharines, Ontario, May 1979).

3. M. Korn, "The Deification of Therapy," *Leisurability* 4, no. 4 (1977): 10–11; J. Levy, "A Comment on Special Events," ibid., no. 1 (1977): 36–37; idem, "A Model for Studying Leisure Behaviour and Mental Health," ibid., no. 3 (1977): 24–26; P. Witt, "Recreational Therapy: Who Cares!" ibid., no. 4 (1977): 13–14.

4. J. Lord, "The Special Olympics: Will Involvement Follow?" *Déficience mentale/ Mental Retardation* 23, no. 4 (1973): 25–27; Levy, "A Comment on Special Events"; idem, "Leisure Behaviour and Mental Health."

5. Lord, "Special Olympics," p. 3.

6. J. F. Murphy and D. R. Howard, *Delivery of Community Leisure Services: An Holistic Approach* (Philadelphia: Lea & Febiger, 1977), p. 170.

The Effects of Patterns of Leisure Behavior in the Shorter Workweek on National Policies

Hana Adoni

During the past few years, government policymakers have repeatedly brought up and discarded the possibility of a five-day workweek. Both private and public corporations have adopted the five-day workweek during this period of deliberation. Within the last year, the subject has won serious attention from policymakers. They have commissioned a number of reports by several experts on various aspects of this issue in order to be able to reach a decision concerning adoption of the five-day workweek.

I was asked by the Ministry of Labor and Social Welfare to prepare a report concerning changes in patterns of leisure resulting from shortening the workweek. Specifically, I was asked to answer two major questions: What changes in time budgeting and leisure patterns of the Israelis can be expected after the institution of the five-day workweek? and What are the potential difficulties inherent in the reallocation of time? I was also asked to prepare basic recommendations for the planning of public policy.

I used several types of data sources to answer these questions. I referred to studies done in Israel on time budgeting and patterns of leisure and to studies on the effects of shortening the workweek in various societies, especially in the United States. I also consulted statistical data that does not deal with

Hana Adoni, Ph.D., is senior lecturer, Communications Institute, the Hebrew University of Jerusalem, Israel.

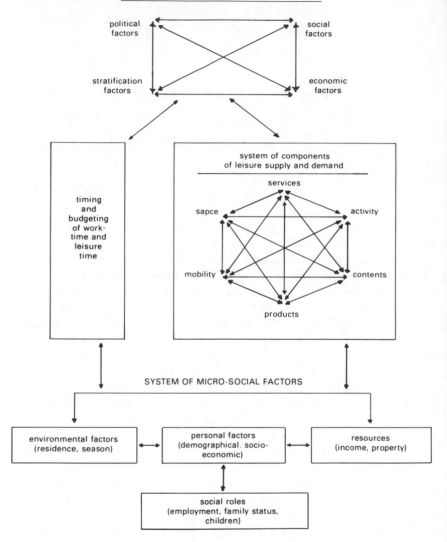

SYSTEM OF MACRO-SOCIAL FACTORS

political factors

social factors

stratification factors

economic factors

timing and budgeting of work-time and leisure time

system of components of leisure supply and demand

services

sapce

activity

mobility

contents

products

SYSTEM OF MICRO-SOCIAL FACTORS

environmental factors (residence, season)

personal factors (demographical. socio-economic)

resources (income, property)

social roles (employment, family status, children)

THE SYSTEMATIC MODEL OF LEISURE

leisure activities but has direct bearing on them; for example, growth in the number of private cars, changes in the consumption of leisure goods and services, and the growing proportion of women working outside the home. Finally, I reviewed a study done by the Ministry of Labor in order to examine changes in several factories that had adopted the five-day workweek.

Before presenting my main conclusions, I would like to refer to the typology of activities I used and to the theoretical conception of the interrelations among different factors concerning changes in leisure patterns. In the literature in the field, the different activities are classified into two main groups: (1) nonleisure activities including gainful employment, housekeeping and shopping, child care, nonleisure travel, and personal needs (such as sleeping, eating, and personal care); and (2) leisure activities including mass-media consumption (such as television, radio, books, papers, and magazines), active sports, leisure travel and outdoor recreation, museums and fairs, entertainment (such as attending movies and listening to pop singers), and cultural events (such as concerts and theater).

At this point I would like to draw your attention to the following theoretical model—the Systematic Model of Leisure. In this model, I have tried to develop a systematic approach to the study of leisure. The literature in the field discusses the various factors appearing in the model. The aim of the model is to illustrate that each group of factors constitutes a subsystem and that each subsystem is a component of the whole system. As such, any change in one subsystem serves as a "triggering mechanism" for changes throughout the whole system. The systematic model can also be applied to what has been termed futuristic research. The model can serve as a conceptual tool for considering alternative scenarios of the future.

An example of the use of the analysis of intersystematic change to chart out alternative futures in the Israeli setting is the question of which day of the week should be chosen as the free day. If Sunday were to be selected, an increased demand

138 LEISURE BEHAVIOR IN THE SHORTER WORKWEEK

for leisure services, transportation, and other facilities would be expected on Saturday night. If, on the other hand, Friday were to be the free day, the pressure on leisure services and facilities would be strongest on Thursday evening and Friday morning, whereas Friday evening would to a large degree retain its present essentially traditional character. Returning to the terms of the model, we can see that two alternatives of time allocation directly influence the components of supply and demand of leisure.

This theoretical model applied to the available data led to certain conclusions and recommendations, which I now offer in some detail.

The shortening of the workweek will primarily affect non-leisure activities, excluding gainful employment. During the additional free day, people will devote more time to such activities as sleeping, eating, housework, shopping, and child care. The reorganization and reallocation of time devoted to these activities will be a function of how the educational system and the public services (including health services and consumer services) are organized. Public and consumer services will have to adapt themselves to the new concentration of free time in one day. The most important factor here is the organization of the educational system, which will have to institute a longer school day because of longer work hours and will have to provide activities to occupy children and youth on the additional free day. Regarding the organization of the educational system, there are two main options: (1) retaining the six-day school week while shortening the teachers' workweek, or (2) shortening the school week to five days and devoting the free day to informal social activities and sports. In my opinion, if the educational system fails to meet this challenge, there could be such negative social consequences as lower levels of academic achievement, especially among deprived young people, and a rise in juvenile delinquency. Furthermore, lower-class mothers of large families will have to bear the burden of deficient educational facilities more than any other social group.

One of the long-term results of shortening the workweek will be an increased amount of time devoted to gainful employment by the population as a whole. This forecast is based on the anticipation of the following changes: *(a)* an increased number of jobs available as a result of the need to compensate those employees who will have to work during the additional free day, *(b)* an increase in overtime work and moonlighting as a result of both the additional free time and the necessity to pay for the new, expensive leisure activities; *(c)* the development of an industry of leisure goods and new leisure services; and *(d)* the addition of a greater number of women to the labor force as a result of flexible work hours and the constant increase in women's level of education.

This analysis of changes in nonleisure activities is particularly relevant to policymakers. They must take into account the social and economic implications of the shortened workweek and decide whether these anticipated changes are compatible with other policy goals. In Israel, for example, the high rate of inflation may be further increased by the greater government spending necessary for the reorganization of the educational system, the development of an infrastructure of leisure services, and the expansion of the labor force in the public sector.

At this point, I would like to present the main conclusions and recommendations concerning patterns of leisure and mass media consumption.

From the data, we can detect several types of changes in the demand for and frequency of leisure activities. If we call the date of institution of the five-day workweek t_1, the different leisure activities can be classified according to changes expected in them in the short run (t_2) and in the long run (t_3).

Type A: Travel, outdoor recreation, movies, and popular entertainment

The frequency of these activities will rise steeply in the short run (t_2), will decrease in the long run (t_3), and will stabilize on a higher level than that prior to t_1. Since this rise can be predicted with a high degree of certainty, the main

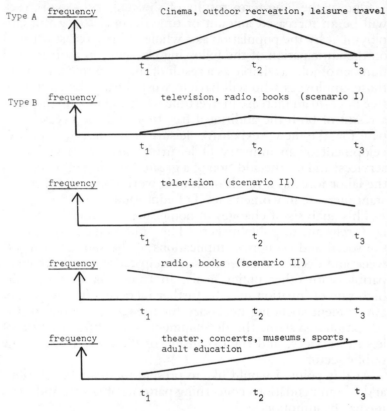

TYPES OF EXPECTED CHANGES IN THE DEMAND FOR AND FREQUENCY OF LEISURE ACTIVITIES IN A SHORTER WORKWEEK IN ISRAEL

recommendation to policymakers is to develop an infrastructure essential for these activities; for example, public parks, beaches, transportation facilities, and resort areas.

Type B: Media consumption

Concerning media consumption, there are two possible scenarios. According to the first scenario, there will be no drastic change in the extent of television broadcasting. In this case, the amount of time devoted to television, reading books and newspapers, and listening to radio and records will not be greatly affected by the shorter workweek, although a slight rise could be expected. According to the second scenario, there will be an additional television channel. In this case, we expect a steep rise in the amount of time devoted to television viewing in the short run (t_2), a slight decrease in the long run (t_3), and stabilization on a slightly higher level of viewing than that prior to t_1.

According to this scenario the consumption of other media will be negatively affected by the increased television viewing in the short run (t_2), but will return to its normal level in the long run (t_3).

Type C: Adult education, theater, concerts, sports, and museums

There will be a gradual rise in the frequency of these activities as a result of an increase in the educational level of the population. In contrast to Type A, a greater increase will occur only if policymakers allocate funds and facilities for the encouragement of participation in these activities.

Although my report to the Ministry of Labor and Social Welfare included a variety of specific recommendations regarding leisure activities, I will discuss them here in a more general sense. The first category of recommendations concerns provision of appropriate leisure facilities for those sectors of the population which have special needs, such as senior citizens and youth. The second category of recommendations deals with the compatibility between the new allocation of time and leisure services and facilities. With the shortening of the workweek, the leisure infrastructure must be expanded and adapted to another free evening and day. The third category of recommendations concerns the role of the mass media in developing a leisure consciousness among the public and in informing the population of available leisure services and facilities. It also includes the possible uses of mass communications for adult education. Research on patterns of leisure in Israel shows that several sectors of the population, especially the lower socioeconomic strata, are not aware of the existing possibilities for active use of leisure time and prefer more passive uses of time such as rest and sleep; but we also know from previous research that a high proportion of Israelis are involved in some type of study in their free time. In my opinion, the mass media and especially television could be used to encourage this tendency. The last category of recommendations suggests encouraging private and public institutions to participate in the planning of leisure activities. For example, school buildings could be used as community centers during evening hours and on weekends.

In conclusion, I would like to refer again to the systematic model of leisure. In my study, I have tried to examine the possible consequences of the change in the allocation of time for leisure and nonleisure activities and to examine the alternative scenarios that could develop as a result of a specific change in one of the components of the system. These alternative directions of development are connected with both the macrocosm (the array of social factors) and the microcosm (the individual). As I mentioned earlier, this study can be seen as an attempt at futuristic research. This type of research does not claim to predict the future, but rather to identify and assess possible alternative futures and to examine their implications for different areas of social action. Within this framework, futuristic research can serve as input for policy decisions made in the present.

One of the main weaknesses of futuristic analysis of leisure patterns is the eclectic data bases. One of my recommendations, therefore, suggests the development of systematic, ongoing research of time budgeting and leisure patterns. The application of futuristic models to the study of leisure aims at increasing the future consciousness, to borrow the phrase from Alvin Toffler, of both policymakers and social scientists interested in the research and planning of leisure.

Changing Work and Leisure Routines: Implications for a Leisure Policy

Richard Kraus

Our very understanding of the meaning of the term *leisure*, and indeed its existence as a phenomenon in society, presupposes the existence of work. We have in recent years made a number of important assumptions about changes occurring in the nature of work and in widely shared attitudes regarding work, which have in turn led to other critical assumptions about the role of leisure in modern life.

There has been general acceptance of the view that work in present-day society is declining steadily, both in terms of its time demands on most people and with respect to the degree of commitment it is able to command from those in the work force. It is a cliché to say that the influence of the so-called Protestant work ethic has declined and that work no longer provides the degree of satisfaction and self-justification that it presumably once did.

Since leisure is generally regarded (at least by most economists and many sociologists) as unobligated time, free of work or maintenance responsibilities, as work declines in volume and importance, leisure logically should expand. We have accepted the principle that, with the decline of work, leisure will increasingly serve to provide meaning and satisfaction in life, an opportunity for creative growth and self-actualization, and a time frame around which to structure our lives. In addition, we have conceptualized the purposeful use of leisure, through organized and sponsored recreational programs, as a strategy

Richard Kraus, Ph.D., is professor and director of the Department of Recreation and Leisure Studies, Temple University, Philadelphia, Pennsylvania, United States.

for attaining certain desirable social goals: the prevention of juvenile delinquency, the strengthening of community ties, the improvement of physical fitness or mental health, and similar objectives.

The specific purpose of this paper is to examine those assumptions and the evidence that supports them. What is happening to work today, in terms of the kind of work that is being done and the schedules or routines that are followed? Who works, and with what degree of commitment? What are the real attitudes that prevail toward work in modern society? To the degree that there is discontent, what modifications are being made to help work become more acceptable or bearable to employees?

Similarly, this paper will examine modern leisure patterns in terms of availability of unobligated time (including projections for the future), as well as in terms of who has leisure and what is being done with it. To what extent is leisure being used to meet needs or values that were formerly work related? What values are being expressed through leisure; how has it been affected by the decline of work; what new expectations do we have of it; and finally, how is it generally perceived in modern society? Is it as a form of social service?

Work Trends Today

Let me begin with the first question—that of changing work routines and involvements. Who works, in what kinds of jobs, and under what time arrangements? The bulk of my remarks in this section will relate only to the economic situation in the United States; however, a number of observations and predictions will apply generally to the other industrialized nations.
The Labor Force

The U.S. Bureau of Labor Statistics has predicted a continuing but gradual rise in the size of the labor force, with an annual rate of increase that declines from almost 2 percent in the late 1970s to slightly more than 1 percent in the 1980s. The American labor force is projected to rise from about 102 million in 1980 to about 108.5 million in 1985 and nearly 114 million in 1990, when the national population is expected to be nearly 245 million.[1] Within this total picture, women will continue to become a larger entity within the work force. Between 1920 and 1970, the percentage of working women rose from 20 percent to 40 percent. Presently more women than men are getting jobs; within a recent twelve-month period, women obtained 55 percent of the 3.3 million new jobs created; it was expected that by 1980, about 50 percent of American women over sixteen years of age would be working. As a long-range prospect, Bednarzik and Klein write:

> Looking ahead . . . development in family formation, fertility, multi-earner families, income needs, educational attainment, and retirement patterns will not reverse the current trends of increasing participation among women and decreasing participation among men.[2]

Nature of Work

It is expected that there will occur a proliferation of so-called knowledge workers, or information specialists, who prepare newsletters, tapes, information transmission materials, and similar products for education, training, and other business uses. In addition, there will be growing needs for systems designers and engineers and greater employment opportunities in fields such as space, solar energy, and ecological engineering. Typists and file clerks will be less in demand as automatic typewriters that take dictation and filing machines that perform routine office work are perfected. In general, however, the long-term trend from blue-collar to white-collar jobs will continue, with farm workers and goods-producing jobs declining, and steady growth in service industries. It has been estimated that by 1985, eight out of every ten workers will be involved in such service fields as information processing, finance, education, communications, health services, and computer-related industries.[3]

As part of this trend, there will continue to be increased use of equipment and machinery that reduces the autonomous, problem-solving or decision-making performance of the worker, and that minimizes his creation of a visible, tangible product, with the concomitant satisfaction and pride that that can bring.

Jobholding Patterns

There has been a steady increase, over the past fifteen years, in part-time employment in the United States. Typically, part-time workers have increased at an annual mean rate of nearly 4 percent, twice the rate of full-time workers. About 22 percent of all nonagricultural employees today are working on a part-time basis.[4]

This trend stems from several causes: *(a)* an increased proportion of working married women or school-aged youth who combine employment with another substantial commitment; *(b)* a Social Security or unemployment insurance system that permits part-time or temporary work in combination with the individual's receiving benefits; *(c)* the growth of service industries that can use part-time workers more efficiently than traditional industrial concerns can (for example, Disney World has several categories of full- and part-time employees, many of whom are available on call, so it can expand or contract its work force to meet seasonal needs); and *(d)* an increased readiness on the part of many young people to commit themselves only partially to work, to meet their minimum economic needs.

It has also been predicted that job sharing, to be discussed later in this paper, will become more prevalent, thus contributing to the number of those holding part-time positions. As far as the converse is concerned—the holding of more than one position—the moonlighting rate has remained fairly constant in recent years. The lowest percentage of multiple jobholding in the work force was 4.5 percent in 1965.[5]

It is also anticipated that accelerated technological changes are likely to bring about a continuing high rate of job obsolescence in the future, phasing out existing jobs and creating new ones. This process will compel many individuals to seek new jobs or to enter second, third, or even fourth career fields during their working lives. To illustrate, comparison of occupational positions showed that about one-third of those employed in 1965 in a given field had shifted to a totally different occupation by 1970. Another survey recently reported in *Psychology Today* showed that nearly two-thirds of those studied anticipated changing jobs within the next five years.[6] Surprisingly, many of those surveyed were older workers who do not normally change jobs so often as younger ones; also, a large number of those surveyed were professionals in fields marked by a high degree of job stability. Much of this pattern of unstable jobholding can be accounted for by marked shifts in the economy, as well as by the continuing migration of many industries in the United States from the North to the Sun Belt.

Available Work and Problems of Unemployment

The question must be asked, What about the future availability of work? Will the predictions that often have been heard about massive unemployment because of increased mechanization and automation or a severe and sustained downslide in the economy be realized?

It should be noted that many of the past predictions in this area have not come true. Automation has not engulfed our economic system so rapidly as forecasts predicted it would, for a variety of reasons: high cost, opposition of labor unions, and lack of technological know-how, as well as the prevailing view that work is necessary and that machines and computers are dehumanizing and should be resisted. It is assumed, however, that in the long run, automation will become increasingly dominant, simply because industrial firms will have to compete with others, and the need to maximize profits will compel them to automate more fully or to simplify their operations by becoming less and less dependent on human performance and more and more reliant on machines.

Although massive unemployment is not predicted for the present century, it seems clear that the chronic problem of a high unemployment or underemployment rate for nonskilled or semiskilled persons, especially minority group members, will continue. It is expected that educational requirements will continue to rise in a number of fields as people with college degrees displace others who are less well educated. For example, between 1970 and 1974, the proportion of workers with college degrees rose by more than 60 percent in clerical, service, and blue-collar occupations. This trend is likely to accelerate due to the relative shortage of jobs; it has been predicted that in the decade preceding 1985 in the United States the number of college graduates will exceed job openings that require college degrees by nearly 950,000.[7]

Looking ahead to the first half of the twenty-first century, it is likely that our society will have to contend more and more with the difficult problem of enforced leisure for a substantial number of members of the work force who can no longer find any work at all for a variety of reasons—automation, inadequate education and skills, or contraction of the job market.

To sum up the points that I have made thus far: (a) there will continue to be a slow increase in the number of jobs, but it is likely that there will be a growing number of unemployed or underemployed individuals; (b) a greater number of positions will be held by women and young workers who tend to accept part-time work; (c) the rate of job change will continue to be high; and (d) jobs themselves will be in the service fields more and more and will tend to rely increasingly on automation, computer equipment, and other machine-related roles that minimize personal creativity and involvement and resultant job satisfaction. These trends tend to support the view that work is likely to become even more unstable or transitory and lacking in the qualities that encouraged the work ethic in the past.

Declining Acceptance of the Work Ethic

Historically, work has been seen as the cornerstone around which man's life was built. Dubin has written:

> It is a commonplace to note that work has long been considered a central life interest for adults in most societies, and certainly in the Western world. Indeed, the capitalist system itself is asserted to rest on the moral and religious justification that the Reformation gave to work.[8]

So strong was the glorification of work as a means of salvation that Max Weber described the Protestant world of being caught in an "iron cage" in which the accepted values were asceticism, restraint, productivity, and harder work for higher profits. The capitalist religion of work thus provided man in the industrialized Western world not only with financial reward but also with a sense of self-respect.[9] Beyond such societal pressures, there have been other important motivations for work. Santayana suggested three obvious ones: want (economic need), ambition (the drive for power), and the love of occupation (intrinsic satisfaction in one's craftsmanship).[10] Dumazedier pointed out that work in a unique human experience, since it "puts man in rapport with materials, with tools and also with other men. Through work he acquires social status."[11]

The tradition of work's being at the moral and religious core of life is no longer widely accepted. Much work today is of a highly specialized, assembly-line nature; since he is not responsible for turning out an entire product, the modern industrial worker rarely has a sense of meaningful involvement with his product. Increasingly, the "instinct of workmanship" has declined on the American scene, and most workers appear to be selling their time rather than taking a deep interest in the job or the enterprise. By the early 1970s, it was apparent that the work ethic had sharply declined.

> In offices and factories, many Americans appear to reject the notion that "labor is good in itself." More and more executives retire while still in their 50's, dropping out of jobs in favor of a life of ease. People who work often take every opportunity to escape. In auto plants, for example, absenteeism has doubled since the early 1960's to five percent of the work force; on Mondays and Fridays it commonly climbs to fifteen percent. In nearly every industry, employees are increasingly refusing overtime work. . . . Beyond that, an increasing number of Americans see no virtue in holding jobs that they consider menial or unpleasant.[12]

A nationwide study of work patterns and attitudes in the United States in the early 1970s revealed that attitudes were rapidly changing on many levels. Yankelovich studied American college youth from 1968 to 1971; although two-thirds of those surveyed professed "mainstream" views in general, their attitudes toward authority were rapidly shifting. In 1968, over half of those surveyed (56 percent) indicated that they did not mind the prospect of being "bossed around" on the job. By 1971, only one out of three students (36 percent) stated that he would be willing to submit to such authority. In 1968, 69 percent of respondents accepted the view that "hard work will always pay off", but in 1971, only 9 percent supported it.[13] Increasing numbers of young people indicated that, while they accepted the idea of work, they saw it ideally in terms of independence, freedom, and risk (in short, with the entrepreneurial spirit of early capitalism) and with a special interest in initiating small business and handicraft ventures rather than being part of large-scale bureaucratic management.

The report, titled *Work in America*, concluded that there was indeed a growing dissatisfaction with present work environments, conditions, and outcomes, for the following reasons: *(a)* the actual decline in the amount of work lessens its impact and its influence on daily life; (a spokesman for the National Manpower Commission recently pointed out that in primitive times, work took up 33 percent of the average person's life span; this dropped to 29 percent in the last century and has since dropped to about 14 percent);[14] *(b)* many young people have higher expectations of work based on their greater education; *(c)* the general level of affluence and job security has made individuals less tolerant of nonrewarding work; *(d)* many workers, including a higher proportion of women employees, have voluntarily joined the work force and are not compelled to work; *(e)* there has been a worldwide pattern, particularly during the 1960s, of challenging the moral authority of established institutions; and *(f)* there is in general more concern about self-actualization, meeting one's creative needs for fuller self-development and satisfaction, in a number of spheres of living.

To illustrate this final point, Yankelovich has recently pointed out that among many young workers, there is a new definition of success that values personal fulfillment and the quality of life as much as it does economic security. According to Yankelovich, many of this "new breed" of younger workers have developed values leading to an insistence that jobs become less depersonalized and placing greater importance on leisure.[15]

Two questions emerge: To what extent has leisure begun to provide the life satisfactions and other values that work no longer offers for many workers? and In what ways have employers attempted to make the work environment and job routines more acceptable to the labor force?

Trends in Amounts and Uses of Leisure

It should not be necessary to document the continued growth of leisure in modern society, although it is helpful to indicate some of the specific forms it has taken and some of the areas of growth projected for the future.

For example, the U.S. Department of Commerce pointed out in its 1977 publication, *Social Indicators*, that leisure time had expanded dramatically for all population groups over a recent ten-year period (1965–75). The increase was most marked for single men—from 36 hours to nearly 45 hours a week. The average number of hours for all adult urban residents rose approximately 11 percent, from 34.8 to 38.5 per week.[16] It should be noted that increases in leisure time have not resulted from sharp declines in the workweek, which has remained relatively stable since World War II. For example, nonagricultural employees worked an average of 38.1 hours in 1975, compared to 40.9 hours in 1948—a modest decline.[17] Instead, the overall increase in leisure has stemmed from such varied sources as the increase in the number of holidays, the growth of paid vacations, and the earlier and more comprehensive retirement of older employees.

Predictions for Future Leisure

In the early 1970s, a group of manpower experts drawn from various disciplines conducted a study supported by the Manpower Administration of the U.S. Department of Labor and agreed that within a decade or two we could look forward to at least several of the following changes:

The average workweek declining to thirty hours; the availability
of thirty-day vacations for at least half of all employees; average
age at retirement being lowered to around sixty years; the number
of employees choosing to work part-time doubling; and the average number of years of education completed rising to two years
beyond high school.[18]

In 1978, the U.S. Chamber of Commerce predicted that
employers should expect a four-day, thirty-two-hour workweek for most workers by the year 2,000, with steady increases in vacation time and holidays also contributing to the
growth of leisure. While there have been other even more
optimistic projections (for example, the prediction by a group
of planners from the Rand Corporation that, with more widespread automation, only 2 percent of the labor force will provide all needed manufactured and agricultural goods for the
entire population), it should be stressed that a number of these
predictions have simply not come true within the time period
described. It should be sufficient to state that the amount of
leisure available to the overall population has grown steadily,
although in a highly differentiated way, with such groups as
working housewives or high-level business executives having
relatively little leisure, and unionized blue-collar or white-
collar employees and, obviously, the unemployed having
much more. All projections indicate that leisure will continue
to grow, and a later section of this paper describes current
efforts to lower the workweek through labor-management
negotiations.

Activities Carried On in Leisure

A typical although misleading approach to describing the
nature of leisure participation in modern society is to cite the
amounts of money spent on various pastimes. For example,
recent compilations suggest that we in the the United States
spend close to $200 billion a year on such activities as travel
and tourism, spectator and participation sports, the fine and
performing arts, entertainment, and such other pleasure-
seeking pursuits as gambling and drinking.

Specifically, recent reports indicate that in 1979 the amount spent on attendance at sporting events rose from $600 million to $1.5 billion; on wheeled vehicles and sports equipment, from $2.8 billion to $9.4 billion; on pari-mutuel betting and racetrack receipts, from $800 million to $1.74 billion; and on gardening, from $1.3 billion to $3.4 billion. Foreign travel is said to involve a record outlay of $12.6 billion a year; television, stereo, radio, and home electronic entertainment units, $5 billion a year.[19] It is worth noting that even during the energy crises and recessions of the early and mid-1970s, leisure spending continued to be extremely high in the United States.[20]

While impressive, such figures do not give us a true or meaningful picture of leisure participation in the United States. Similarly, reports that highlight the popularity of such activities as skin and scuba diving, disco dancing, hang gliding, or even skiing and tennis tend to give somewhat exaggerated impressions of the actual popularity of such pursuits among the population at large. Specific surveys of sample populations are somewhat more useful in this regard. For example, a recent survey by the U.S. Department of the Interior shows the relative popularity of various outdoor activities performed at least five times a year:

walking or jogging	96.8	million	participants
picnicking	84	"	"
pool swimming	83.5	"	"
bicycling	66	"	"
fishing	62	"	"
nature walks	62	"	"
beach swimming	59	"	"
tennis	41	"	"
boating	34	"	"
off-road vehicles	34	"	"
hiking	38	"	"
hunting	24	"	"

In another recent poll of a large population sample, carried out by ABC News and the Harris Survey organization,[22] the most popular activities were identified as shown in the table below. How is one to assess these two reports? In general, they affirm what we have known for some time—that although considerable attention is given in the press to leisure activities that are faddish, unusual, or of a high-risk nature, most people engage on a day-by-day, week-by-week basis in activities that

MOST POPULAR LEISURE ACTIVITIES IN THE USA, 1979

LEISURE-TIME ACTIVITIES		PARTICIPATION	
	Frequently	Occasionally	Seldom or Not at All
Eating	54%	30%	16%
Watching television	41	34	25
Listening to the radio	40	34	26
Reading books	39	27	34
Listening to music at home	39	37	24
Fixing things around the house	36	36	28
Social activities	25	41	34
Having sex	25	41	34
Church or club activities	23	20	57
Outdoor activities	21	26	53
Hobbies	20	20	60
Sports	19	22	59
Earning extra money	17	21	62
Continuing education	15	16	69
Getting away for change of scenery	15	44	41
Taking naps	14	27	59
Just doing nothing	13	24	63
Attending spectator sports	13	25	62
Playing cards or games	12	26	62
Volunteer work	11	18	71
Artistic pursuits	9	11	80
Going to the movies	8	31	61
Playing a musical instrument	7	8	85
Attending theater, music, or dance performances	6	23	71
Disco dancing	5	9	86
Political activities	4	11	85
Gambling	2	9	89

are routine, simple, safe, inexpensive, casual, and close to home. By far the most popular activities are those which require no special equipment, sponsorship, knowledge, or abilities. Indeed, such homely activities as eating, watching television, reading, or fixing things around the home are strikingly popular, compared to other, more clearly recognizable or active recreational pastimes.

These reports suggest a logical question that is highly germane to the assumptions outlined at the beginning of this paper: To what extent can such time-wasting, trivial, or relatively undemanding and casual activities provide satisfaction and reward of a significant nature? The character of the most popular activities suggests that they are carried on for fun, sociability, or simply to pass the time, but not to achieve a fuller sense of self or to meet important challenges or commitments. To gain a fuller perspective on this issue, it is necessary to look at recent research done in the area of the psychology of leisure.

Research in the Psychology of Leisure

In recent years, a growing body of research has emerged that explores not so much the kinds of activities engaged in, in relation to socioeconomic variables (as in earlier research), but rather the meaning and affective values attached to leisure participation today.

For example, a considerable number of studies have been carried out in the specialized area of sports psychology. The motivation of athletes, the development of team morale, the nature of group dynamics and team leadership, the personality traits of athletes, self-actualization and self-concept among athletes, and other psychological aspects of sports participation have been the subject of numerous articles in *Research Quarterly* by such investigators as Morgan,[23] O'Connor and Webb,[24] Ibrahim and Morrison,[25] and Martin and Myrick.[26]

Within the broader realm of leisure involvement and attitudes, Neulinger and Crandall point out that we are no longer satisfied to *name* the activities people engage in; we want to know what they *mean* to the participants. Especially as a humanistic and holistic approach to leisure becomes more fully accepted, psychological analysis of leisure involvement will contribute to our planning and policy making in this field. They write:

> A psychological definition of leisure . . . emphasizing self-development and fulfillment through freely chosen, meaningful activities, makes leisure particularly relevant and valuable for those sections of our society that are presently underprivileged in one way or another.[27]

Several studies in the 1970s began to explore such theoretical questions as the relationships between leisure participation and personality, the influence of parental values and early play experiences on later choices, and similar dimensions of leisure participation. For example, in a report, "Work Orientation, Meaning of Leisure and Mental Health," Spreitzer and Snyder explored a compensatory hypothesis—that when work did not permit self-actualization and self-expression, leisure would tend to take on enriched meaning as a form or source of self-definition.[28] Their data supported the conclusion that people who lacked an intrinsic involvement with their jobs would be more likely to define their leisure activities as a means of self-identity. However, they also concluded that there was a modest but consistent association between the tendency to define leisure activities as a source of self-identity, on one hand, and poor psychological adjustment, on the other; in other words, those who rely on leisure as a means of strengthening their own self-concepts tend to be poorly adjusted psychologically. Similarly, their findings suggest that the working world continued to be so important to the subjects of their research that the degree of satisfaction they received from their jobs was a key factor in their general state of happiness and satisfaction with life. Although they reported that their data suffered from a number of confounding variables related to the level of work, and recommended that further research be carried out in this area, Spreitzer and Snyder concluded that although one's leisure activities

> may compensate for job dissatisfaction, our data suggest that they frequently are not a satisfactory substitute since leisure activities do not appear to be as psychologically encompassing as a self-actualizing work experience.[29]

A second piece of research aimed at exploring the relationship between leisure and work was carried out by Kelly at the University of Illinois and reported in *Society and Leisure*.[30] Kelly outlined two contrasting approaches to conceptualizing this relationship: *(a)* the *dualist* view, which sees leisure as a separate area or sphere of human activity that is independent of work and related aspects of the social milieu; and *(b)* the *holistic* view, which sees the possibility of work influencing leisure in such a way as to make leisure an extension of work roles and orientations, or a recovery from work intended to make the employee fit for more work. Extending this analysis, Kelly suggested a definitional paradigm of leisure based on two key variables: societal constraints and pressures, and degree of work relatedness. He identified four ways of defining leisure based on these variables:

1. Unconditional leisure: carried on for its own sake, and for intrinsic satisfaction, with a minimum of expectations related to family or community values
2. Coordinated leisure: freely chosen, but similar to the participant's involvement in work, in form or content
3. Complementary leisure: strongly influenced by work, family, or community role expectations; may be either role-related (similar to work) or compensatory (contrasting with work)
4. Required activity carried on in nonwork time: not really regarded as leisure, but done to prepare for work, maintain household, etc.

Based on a study of an adult population's participation in

344 different activities in nonwork time, Kelly found that almost 90 percent of the activities engaged in had either unconditional or complementary orientations. However, he found little support for the view that leisure was strongly influenced by work or intended to compensate for the lack of work satisfaction. The family context was apparently the most influential in determining the choice of leisure activities, and the intrinsic satisfaction found in the activity itself was the primary reason for participation. He concluded:

> Leisure orientations and decision premises of those . . . studied here are neither integrated with their work nor seem to be determined by it. Rather, leisure seems to be an arena of life that is separate from work. Leisure is part of the non-work world of family and community roles and expectations, especially for those whose leisure is given a focus by their parental roles and responsibilities.[31]

Based on the popular literature, it is possible to suggest that the increasing numbers of people who engage in challenging or demanding kinds of leisure, activities such as high-risk outdoor activities or serious cultural involvements, do so to provide the same kinds of satisfactions that absorbing work can provide. There is no evidence, however, that those who do so are attempting, either consciously or unconsciously, to compensate for the lack of enjoyable or rewarding work. Indeed, it might very well be that the same individuals who are involved in demanding and meaningful work are those who also engage in hobbies or cultural interests that also provide deep satisfactions; and similarly, that individuals with boring, mechanical jobs tend to use their leisure in time-wasting and superficial ways. No research has been discovered that would support this hypothesis.

Other elements linking work and leisure are discussed in the popular or scholarly literature on recreation and leisure. It is apparent that many individuals tend to make their leisure worklike by transferring to it all the compulsive attitudes with which they approach their work. Whether it is simply that people require structure, a sense of order, or the reassurance that they are involved in significant forms of time commitment, such individuals tend to "work" at their play and to surround themselves with a host of obligations that take away any possible sense of leisurely enjoyment, relaxation, or creative self-development. As Walter Kerr has written in *The Decline of Pleasure:*

> We are all of us compelled to read for profit, party for contacts, lunch for contracts, bowl for unity, drive for mileage, gamble for charity, go out for the evening for the greater glory of the municipality, and stay home for the weekend to rebuild the house.[32]

Typically, in the life of the organization man or woman, leisure may be deliberately used as a way to build business contacts, cultivate the "right" people, make sales, or build an image of oneself that is useful in furthering one's career. For many individuals, as Alexander Reid Martin has pointed out, leisure becomes an almost insurmountable challenge. These individuals—frequently successful professionals or business executives—have what Martin describes as a weekend neurosis. Able to function effectively within the framework of a job, where goals are clear and there is little ambiguity, they often cannot deal with the threat of leisure. Nervous breakdowns, heart attacks, and many forms of acute psychosomatic illness are all too likely to occur during free time; many so-called workaholics simply are unwilling to schedule themselves for holidays or vacations for long periods of time.

In contrast with this, a growing number of individuals in modern society have accepted the challenge of personal self-actualization through leisure, to the degree that they deliberately reject work, except as a means to an end (that of minimal financial self-support) and make their lives, in effect, an unending round of hobbies and leisure pursuits. For them, leisure represents the key element in their life-style, and they move from place to place, engaging in sports and games, snow skiing, water skiing, surfing, mountain climbing, driving off-road vehicles, and frequently developing associations with others who share their interests. Retired individuals who live in travel trailers and go South in the winter and North in the summer, backpacking enthusiasts, scuba divers, antique hobbyists, swamp buggy racers, body builders, craftsmen and craftswomen, snowmobile racers, skydivers, folk music performers and fans, tailgating party goers at professional football games, collectors, artifact searchers who use metal detectors, mummy dusters who volunteer in archaeological museums, hang gliders, performers in little theaters, people who practice "creative anachronism" (enacting lives of past or mythical cultures)—all illustrate such absorbing hobbies.[33]

Sometimes their interests are prompted by community tradition or the efforts of a local chamber of commerce to promote the image of a region or town, as in the proliferation of festivals, contests, and other events that absorb hundreds of participants in varied, time-consuming activities. Not infrequently, they seem deliberately to involve a repudiation of seriousness itself. In their leisure, people sometimes seek out activities that are ridiculous or "far out" in their very nature—such as turkey racing, chicken plucking, frog jumping, baby crawling, barhopping, "polar bear" swim meets, or demolition derbies on frozen lakes.[34] Participants in such activities are, in effect, thumbing their noses at society's work-oriented, materialistic, and practical values and saying, "See me! I'm weird—and I like it." While such individuals clearly define themselves in terms of their leisure rather than their work, it seems understandable that they are likely to appear poorly adjusted on standard psychological tests, given the probable bias of these tests.

Although research evidence is lacking, there is clearly a general trend among young people to value work less, to do less of it, and to choose occupations that are in some way playlike or creative in nature. According to a spokesman for the National Manpower Commission, studies have shown that only one of five persons today says that work means more to him as a source of satisfaction than leisure. Sixty percent of those questioned say that, although they like their work, it is not their main source of satisfaction.[35]

Changing Work Routines

Recognizing that worker boredom and lack of commitment have been responsible for increasing absenteeism, careless performance, accidents, problems related to drug use and drinking on the job, and even in some cases deliberate sabotage, employers in both Europe and America have made deliberate efforts to transform work so that it will be more acceptable and satisfying. In some cases, the task itself, or the social framework in which it is carried on, have been altered. In others, the scheduling has been changed to permit greater flexibility and often fuller use of leisure time.

Efforts to Make Work More Interesting

Particularly in northern Europe and the Scandinavian countries, large-scale manufacturing concerns have made serious attempts to make work more interesting and less routine and monotonous. One method has been to provide the worker with more varied roles or alternating assignments in order to provide variety. In some cases, workers or teams of workers have been given freedom to make decisions regarding their tasks and feel, therefore, a larger sense of involvement in the final product. Some experiments have involved setting work goals for the day or week and letting teams of workers themselves decide the pace or sequence by which they will achieve the goals, rather than having a typical assembly-line, automatic rate of work.

Any such changes must be considered within the framework of a society's prevailing business philosophy. Heretofore in the industrial world, emphasis has been placed on utility, expediency, and efficiency. In effect, the worker has been fitted to the machine and the bureaucratic social structures, with clearly defined authority, rules, and procedures, along with highly specialized job tasks and inflexible routines, which have characterized most large-scale manufacturing situations.

Given the climate of developing opposition to authority and centralized control and the new emphasis on the quality of life and fulfillment of one's creative potential, many companies have radically altered their prevailing philosophy, resulting in the kinds of job changes just described. This has obviously been somewhat easier to do in service industries, which tend to rely more heavily on individual effort and problem solving, than in manufacturing concerns. On all levels, however, it would appear that the trend is toward providing an environment in which creativity and flexibility are stressed, as opposed to rigid and bureaucratic work routines.

New Scheduling Approaches

A second trend has been toward new kinds of work schedules, including variations of the workweek, flex-time, and job sharing.

As indicated earlier, the workweek has remained fairly stable for the past three decades, although a coalition of labor unions has recently begun serious efforts in the United States to reduce it to thirty-two hours.[36] While a minority of workers would probably use the free time thus gained for moonlighting in second jobs, it seems likely that the majority would make use of it for leisure activities. A recent survey, for example, reported that a high percentage of surveyed workers indicated willingness to sacrifice a portion of their income in exchange for longer vacations and more flexible work periods.[37]

In addition to shortening the workweek, there have been numerous efforts to alter it by breaking away from the common five-day pattern. During the 1960s, numerous companies experimented with the three-day and four-day workweek, and for a time it seemed as if the four-day workweek, with ten hours of work a day, would become widely adopted. However, this arrangement, which clearly would make much larger blocks of time available for leisure activity, has not achieved wide acceptance among American companies. While it is uniquely suited to some types of manufacturing cycles, it does not suit other industries well, and in general it has been resisted by unions because in their eyes the ten-hour day represents a return to earlier and outdated labor policies.

A somewhat more widely accepted approach to varying work routines in order to provide increased flexibility and worker satisfaction involves a concept known as flex-time.

Typically, this arrangement permits workers to be on the job for eight hours within an overall twelve-hour period. For example, on any given day, employees might begin work between 6:30 A.M. and 9:30 A.M. and end between 3:00 P.M. and 6:00 P.M., with the core period being between 9:00 *a.m.* and 3:00 P.M. Both private and government agencies have adopted the flex-time system; recently the Social Security Administration in suburban Washington extended this option to 25,000 employees. Among the advantages of flex-time are: *(a)* it gives workers greater freedom in arranging their daily schedules, sharing time with their families, and carrying out needed chores; *(b)* by spreading commuting hours more widely, it helps to reduce rush-hour traffic congestion; *(c)* it reduces boredom and frustration by giving workers a degree of choice in their work schedules, allowing for different lifestyles; *(d)* it treats employees like adults and enhances their feelings of freedom and autonomy; and *(e)* it eliminates lateness as a problem (because employees may arrive later but must complete their full days) and cuts down on absenteeism.

Both in the United States and in Europe, flex-time is a rapidly growing way of work; since the mid-1970s, the number of firms in the United States using it has doubled, and an estimated 6 percent of all American employees now have it as an option, not counting the self-employed and others who traditionally set their own hours. Like the four-day workweek, flex-time gives the worker considerable freedom in arranging his leisure hours.

A third approach that has been growing rapidly involves job sharing. This is best suited to smaller, more flexible companies or organizations, which tend to be less bureaucratic in nature. In some cases, job sharing, which involves two or more workers holding part-time jobs, has been initiated by labor unions, as in the case of the electrical workers in New York City who have deliberately rotated layoffs made necessary by a slow job market. In a number of states, particularly California, full-time positions in schools, libraries, and other agencies have been split to allow job sharing.

The advantages of this system are: *(a)* it reduces unemployment by sharing the available work; *(b)* it increases job opportunities for people who are unable to hold full-time jobs, such as parents with young children or the handicapped; *(c)* it eases certain transitions, such as housewife to full-time worker or worker to retiree; *(d)* it permits midcareer training without a total loss of income; and *(e)* it reduces absenteeism and makes possible a more precise tailoring of the labor supply to the needs of employers.

Business Sponsorship of Recreation Programs

Still another link between work and leisure lies in the arrangement under which many companies have begun to provide recreation as a service. Obviously, this happens most frequently as a form of commercial enterprise; thousands of companies manufacture leisure goods and equipment and provide entertainment, instruction, and a host of other recreational opportunities.

Furthermore, many companies have moved into the role of recreation provider for their own employees. In the mid-1970s, it was reported that 50,000 private companies were spending $2 billion a year on recreation-related programs, with over 800 of the largest of these companies belonging to the National Industrial Recreation Association. The rationale for such programs is obvious: employers seek to improve company-employee relations; to build a sense of loyalty to the company; to improve employee efficiency by reducing emotional strains stemming from boredom, frustration, or alcohol or drug use; and to enhance the image of the company, as well as its ability to recruit needed personnel, through a wide range of employee benefits. As a consequence, such large companies as IBM, the Xerox Corporation, Johnson & Johnson, and other banking, insurance, and manufacturing concerns operate large-scale country clubs or recreation centers for their employees and offer courses, clubs, sports leagues, charter travel opportunities, and numerous other recreational activities, often geared for family participation.

As a special aspect of such programs, there has been a trend toward offering executive fitness programs (involving medical testing and supervision, jogging, exercise machines, and racket sports) to promote the health and fitness of upper-echelon employees, who are notably vulnerable to tension, stress, and cardiovascular disease; however, they also tend to have a recreational aspect and thus to meet leisure values as well. There is an increasing recognition that business executives should develop the nonbusiness side of their lives. The leading authority on management theory and staff development, Peter Drucker, urges them to move out of the realm of the specialized business world, to develop amateur interests and cultural activities, in order to enrich both their own lives and the "society of organizations." He writes:

> Precisely because so much of his time and interest is preoccupied with his organization's "public" life, the manager needs a private life with different concerns, different values and above all different personal ties and different friendships. . . . To be viable, let alone to be enjoyable, a society of organizations needs cultures that are personal rather than managerial, that are diverse and pluralistic. It needs a counter-culture of amateurs.[38]

This view was reinforced by an extensive longitudinal study of graduates of Harvard College over a thirty-year period—men who have in striking numbers become best-selling novelists and cabinet members, scholars and captains of industry, physicians and teachers of the first rank, judges and newspaper editors, and leaders including the late President John F. Kennedy. The researchers found that in predicting future success, the individual's original social class was unimportant; instead, his social adjustment and degree of being well organized, practical, and well integrated as a human being meant everything. The key to successful adjustment was the ability to play, as evidenced by the ability to engage in competitive games, such as tennis with friends, and to take long and imaginative vacations from work.[39]

More and more, then, leading authorities on business and the work world are coming to recognize the importance of creative and constructive uses of leisure and are assigning recreation a higher degree of priority in their own lives.

National Priorities Linking Work and Leisure

Leisure has been viewed as an important societal concern since the time of the Greek philosophers Plato and Aristotle. During the past several centuries, the tendency has been to view leisure in two diametrically opposed ways: as an opportunity and as a social menace. Obviously, leisure has been seen as providing the means for enriching culture, strengthening community life, building desirable human relationships, and contributing to the physical and mental health of participants. On the other hand, it has also been viewed as a danger—the opportunity for drunkeness, vice, violence, crime, or values antithetical to the established societal mores to take over.

This can best be illustrated by the Soviet Union's approach to the leisure "problem." During the 1920s and 1930s, every aspect of Soviet life, including recreation and leisure, was regarded as part of a collective scheme to build national morale, improve health, and increase productivity. The concept of leisure within the Soviet Union was closely linked to the promotion of "socialist discipline" and the development of community solidarity and a common morality. Whetten wrote:

> Leisure activities are vitally important in a controlled society. Unless leisure time is carefully regulated, the "sense of sacrifice" which the worker is taught on the job could desert him in the hours he is away from it. . . . Realization of the state's ultimate goal thus depends, at least in part, on its success in controlling leisure time.[40]

The early Soviet concept of leisure was that it should be used by workers to "rest and gather strength for new labors and success." Thus, the Russians developed an elaborate system of rest homes and vacation resorts for workers. Other Soviet provisions for leisure included a system of day-care centers and summer camps for children, Pioneer Youth Palaces or recreation and cultural centers, and numerous clubs, societies, and sports programs for adults. Extensive parks, stadiums, wintersports facilities, and cultural programs have provided a means of strengthening and enriching the use of leisure within an approved set of national values and objectives. Typically, government officials have been concerned about the invasion of Western "decadence" in the form of "immoral entertainment"; frequent drives are conducted against the importation of rock 'n' roll dancing and music and of foreign films, publications, and art. A leading sociologist, G. S. Petrosian, warned that free time must not lead to idleness: "It is the time devoted to study, the raising of [occupational] qualifications, self-education and self-development." *Pravda* expressed the government's position:

> To care about the cultural recreation of the people is above all to ensure the conditions making it possible for the working people to spend their free time in such a way as to raise their general cultural and professional level to improve [themselves] physically and aesthetically.[41]

Nonetheless, leisure continues to constitute a major problem in the Soviet Union. Despite government efforts to provide constructive activities, many young people in particular seek diversions of the sort found in American society, often in defiance of the establishment.[42] Marital breakup has become increasingly common, alcoholism is a growing concern, and workers express their boredom and resentment against poor working conditions by absenteeism and drinking on the job.[43] Thus, even in a controlled society, leisure continues to constitute a problem. This is particularly true in the smaller industrial towns and remote regions of the Soviet Union:

> "Life is boring here." But nothing seems to alleviate the problem. A major reason is the pervasive dullness of life in provincial Soviet cities. Workers at an industrial rubber-goods plant in the central

Asian republic of Kazakhstan wrote *Pravda:* "Life is boring here. Just think of a town that has no clubs, no movie theatre, no stadium. After a day's work, there is nothing to do, and because of this some are attracted to drinking."[44]

Within the Western world, a major portion of leisure is filled by businesses that provide recreation commercially, in the form of varied amusements, entertainments, and other leisure-time products. Government itself provides constructive activity, in the form of outdoor recreation, cultural activity, community center programs, municipal parks, playgrounds and sports programs, and a host of other opportunities. Nonetheless, here as within the Soviet Union, there are obvious problems. Most of the available activities require expenditures that restrict the participation of disadvantaged groups in society. Special populations, such as the physically or mentally disabled and the aged, are frequently barred from most commercial and many public recreation programs by architectural barriers or by a lack of mobility, funds, or knowledge.

What is needed is a set of policies, shared by the major leisure-serving agencies in society (government, education, voluntary, private, and commercial organizations) that will do the following:

1. Determine an appropriate set of priorities or needs to be met, with respect to the provision of leisure opportunities for various age groups or socioeconomic classes in society. For example, the needs of youth tend to be quite different from those of the aged, and leisure policies should therefore have different emphases or objectives for each group.

2. Survey, much more effectively than has been done in the past, how these needs are presently being met. Most such efforts in the past have simply measured what people do, rather than examine the contributions made by various types of agencies within the complex, interlocking system of leisure opportunity. Based on such an examination, an appropriate set of leisure respon-

sibilities or functions could be defined for municipal
governments, voluntary agencies, the schools, and other
organizations with a stake in this problem.
3. Develop opportunity models with various population
   groups, as suggested above, and provide adequate
   facilities and programs to meet the needs that have been
   identified.
4. Develop a national awareness of the problem of leisure
   and its importance for community life and physical,
   mental, and social well-being. This can best be done
   through a system of leisure education and, in special
   cases, leisure counseling, and should be applied not only
   to children and youth, but also to other age groups,
   including the elderly, who frequently have a serious
   problem of adjustment to retirement because of a lack of
   appropriate leisure attitudes and resources.
5. Continue to attempt to break down the existing
   dichotomy between work and leisure, so that both can
   be seen as contributing to the quality of life and to meeting fundamental human needs. Ideally, work and the
   work environment can be changed so that they become
   psychologically rewarding to most of the work force; at
   the same time, with a new perception of leisure and its
   significance in modern life and society, workers will be
   able to use their growing amounts of free time in meaningful and creative ways, rather than with guilt or in
   passive and superficial ways.

NOTES

1. Howard N. Fullerton and Paul O. Flaim, "New Labor Force Projections to
1990," *Monthly Labor Review* 99 (1976): 3–13.
   2. Robert W. Bednarzik and Deborah P. Klein, "Labor Force Trends: A Synthesis
and Anaylysis," *Monthly Labor Review* 100 (1977): 3–11.
   3. "Americans Change," *Business Week*, 20 February 1978, pp. 64–69.
   4. William V. Deuterman and Scott C. Brown, "Voluntary Part-Time Workers: A
Growing Part of the Labor Force," *Monthly Labor Review* 101 (1978): 3–10.
   5. William Abbott, "Work in the Year 2001," *Futurist* 11 (1977): 25–31.
   6. Patricia A. Renwick and Edward E. Lawler, "What You Really Want from
Your Job," *Psychology Today* 11 (1978): 53–65, 118.

7. *Business Week*, 20 April 1978, n.p.

8. Robert Dubin, "Industrial Workers' Worlds," in Eric Larrabee and Rolf Meyersohn, eds., *Mass Leisure* (Glencoe, Ill.: Free Press, 1958), p. 215.

9. For a fuller discussion, see Nels Anderson, *Work and Leisure* (New York: Free Press, 1961).

10. Ibid., p. 26.

11. Ibid., p. 26.

12. "Is the Work Ethic Going Out of Style?" *Time*, 30 October 1972, p. 96.

13. Special Task Force to the Secretary of HEW, *Work in America* (Cambridge, Mass.: MIT Press, 1973), p. 44.

14. Fred Best, National Manpower Commission, cited in Jonathan Wolman, "The Future of Working: Less of It for More of Us," *Philadelphia Inquirer*, 3 September 1978.

15. Daniel Yankelovich, "The New Psychological Contracts at Work," *Psychology Today* 11 (1978):46–50.

16. "Big Changes in How People Live," *U.S. News and World Report*, 16 January 1978, p. 42.

17. John D. Owen, "Work Weeks and Leisure: An Analysis of Trends, 1948–1975," *Monthly Labor Review* 99 (1976):3–7.

18. Burt Nanus and Harvey Adelman, "Forecast for Leisure" in *Leisure Today: Selected Readings* (Washington, D.C.: American Association for Leisure and Recreation, 1975), p. 30.

19. "Leisure: Where No Recession Is in Sight," *U.S. News and World Report*, 15 January 1979, pp. 41–43.

20. Philip Shabecoff, "Leisure Activities Thrive in Recession," *New York Times*, 1 May 1975.

21. Cited in "Leisure: Where No Recession Is in Sight," p. 43.

22. "Leisure Survey Results Released," American Association for Leisure and Recreation *Reporter*, April 1979, pp. 1, 3.

23. William P. Morgan, "Selected Psychological Considerations in Sport," *Research Quarterly*, December 1974, pp. 374–89.

24. Kathleen A. O'Connor and James L. Webb, "Investigation of Personality Traits of College Female Athletes and Non-athletes," *Research Quarterly*, March 1976, pp. 203–10.

25. Hilmi Ibrahim and Nettie Morrison, "Self-Actualization and Self-Concept among Athletes," *Research Quarterly*, March 1976, pp. 68–79.

26. Warren S. Martin and Fred L. Myrick, "Personality and Leisure Time Activities," *Research Quarterly*, May 1976, pp. 246–53.

27. John Neulinger and Rick Crandall, "The Psychology of Leisure," *Journal of Leisure Research*, August 1976, pp. 181–84.

28. Elmer A. Spreitzer and Eldon E. Snyder, "Work Orientation, Meaning of Leisure and Mental Health," *Journal of Leisure Research*, Summer 1974, pp. 207–19.

29. Ibid., p. 218.

30. John R. Kelly, "Leisure Decisions: Exploring Extrinsic and Role-Related Orientations," *Society and Leisure*, 1975, no. 4, pp. 45–61.

31. Ibid., p. 58.

32. Walter Kerr, *The Decline of Pleasure* (New York: Simon & Schuster, 1965), p. 39.

33. See Mark Jury, *Playtime: Americans at Leisure* (New York: Harcourt, Brace, Jovanovich, 1977).

34. Ibid.

35. Jonathan Wolman, "The Future of Working: Less of It for More of Us," *Philadelphia Inquirer*, 3 September 1978.

36. Ibid.

37. Fred Best, "Preferences in Worklife Scheduling and Work-Leisure Tradeoffs," *Monthly Labor Review* 101 (1978): 31–37.

38. Peter F. Drucker, "Memo to Managers: Find Outside Pleasure," *New York Times*, 5 May 1974.

39. George E. Vaillant, *Adaptations to Life* (New York: Little, Brown, 1977).

40. Lawrence, Whetten, "Leisure in the Soviet Union," *Recreation*, February 1961, p. 91.

41. Quoted in "Modern Living: Discovering the Weekend in Russia," *Time*, 9 May 1969, p. 73.

42. David K. Shipler, "A Problem for Soviet's Young: What to Do with Leisure," *New York Times*, 16 December 1977.

43. David K. Willis, "Soviet Divorce Rate Climbs: Alcohol and New Roles Cited," *Philadelphia Inquirer*, 16 March 1978.

44. Robin Knight, "Why Workers Want to Flee U.S.S.R.," *U.S. News and World Report*, 29 May 1978, p. 58.

Leisure: A State of Mind That All Desire but Few Achieve

John Neulinger

Perhaps the most amazing fact about this international seminar on molding leisure policies taking place in Jerusalem, Israel in 1979 is the fact that it is taking place. It not only expresses a sense of confidence in the state of the nation, but also a unique recognition of the importance of leisure for its well-being. "It is a good state if it fosters leisure."[1] We all have reason to rejoice: Israel, at least, has recognized the value of leisure. It has included it among its primary goals. Or has it?

In preparation for this conference, we were given the opportunity to become familiar with a most informative and relevant book on Israel: *The Secularization of Leisure: Culture and Communication in Israel.*[2] It is reasonable to assume that this work gives a fair representation of the predominant conception of leisure in this country. A careful reading indicated that the term *leisure* was used consistently (an amazing consistency, compared to most American works!) in the sense of "free time." Is it, then, free, unobligated, discretionary time that we attribute all this importance to? Surely not. But if not free time, per se, perhaps it is the content of free time that is the crucial ingredient. The very first sentence of *The Secularization of Leisure* speaks of "leisure [free time] and cultural activities." And somewhat later the authors point out that "the Jews invented leisure (in the institution of the Sabbath) and then took

John Neulinger, Ph.D., is professor, Department of Psychology, the City College of the City University of New York, New York, United States.

it back again by minutely prescribing how to spend it."[3] Content again! It is the content of leisure (free time) that seems to justify the importance of leisure (free time).

We are confronting here an issue that goes far beyond being a semantic problem. It is the leisure–free time distinction, the difference between a sociological (objective, residual) and a psychological (subjective, state of mind) conception. Disentangling this confusion was one of the principal concerns of de Grazia's *Of Time, Work and Leisure*.[4] I have elaborated on this issue extensively elsewhere,[5] and will raise here only questions that are directly relevant to this conference. I want to take the position that leisure, understood as a state of mind, is valuable regardless of content. Content may be qualitatively related to the experience of leisure, but its critical components are certain essential conditions (for example, psychological variables)—primarily that of perceived freedom.[6]

De Grazia depicted such a view of leisure, except that he was pessimistic as to human nature: "Leisure refers to a state of being, a condition of man, which few desire and fewer achieve."[7] As the title of this paper suggests, I shall argue for a more positive view and suggest that leisure is a state that is universally desired, although not necessarily universally achieved.

First, a clarification. I want to be sure not to be misunderstood. It is not my intention to prescribe how anyone should define leisure. The term has been used in three quite distinct ways: as a period of time (free time), as an activity (free-time activity), and as a state of mind (an experience). Each of these domains has its own problems and approaches and needs to be investigated in order to arrive at appropriate policy suggestions. The important point is that we are clear when we do use the label *leisure*.

The study of leisure as free time has been the domain of the traditional sociological approach. Katz and Gurevitch, as has been pointed out, very consistently follow that line, and consequently and in line with the prevailing tradition, emphasize content, namely, cultural activities.[8] The importance of leisure, however, is derived from the nature of the content that becomes available to people within that free time. The task of the leisure policymaker is, first, one of providing enough free time and, then, filling it up with activities that have been judged appropriate and perhaps even "useful" in terms of societal values.

Another major implication of this orientation is that we are restricted to only part of the person's life. We are concerned with certain time periods and not with others, such as work time, time spent on household matters, and so on. A state-of-mind approach does not allow or necessitate such a splitting of the person. An experience does exist in time; after all, everything does. But time, per se, is not a relevant dimension. Perhaps the best way to characterize the leisure experience and to illustrate at the same time "the absurdity of this phrase 'leisure-time'" is to use Green's analogy of love.[9] Love is a condition of the mind, not a category of time. You either love your child or you do not; but certainly you do not just love your child from 9:00 to 9:15 in the morning, or from 12:00 to 2:00 in the afternoon, or during the weekend.

The orientation of this paper and my general approach to leisure is of this type—leisure as a state of mind. I have described elsewhere the conditions I see as essential for the generation of the leisure experience, namely, perceived freedom and intrinsic motivation.[10] Since this conference is primarily concerned with policy formation, I shall restrict myself here to a discussion of the implications of a psychological conception of leisure.

Leisure: A Universal Goal

The most important implication of a state-of-mind conception of leisure is not just the fact that we make it clear that we are dealing with an experiential phenomenon, but that the state we are referring to is a universally desired one.[11] It is the state of mind emerging from the perception of freedom and involvement in intrinsically motivated activities. These are the conditions that lead one to perceive oneself as being an origin rather than a pawn—a desire that overrides all other motives.[12]

They involve behavior that makes a person feel competent and self-determined;[13] they are necessary conditions to engage in the search for meaning, a core motivational propensity common to all;[14] they are essential to the perception of flow.[15] In short, these are the conditions underlying the need for and fulfillment of being rather than having.[16]

Are there individuals who would want to avoid such experiences and thus these conditions? Who would rather not be free, not be an origin, not be self-determined? Of course, there are such individuals. We all are aware of *Escape from Freedom*,[17] the syndrome of "Sunday Neurosis,"[18] and the fact that addicts tend to seek structure rather than autonomy.[19] The fact that intrapersonal conflicts in regard to freedom may occur does not preclude the potential universal desire for freedom. We do not deny the universality of the life instinct just because we might also accept the death instinct. The only implication of all this is the increased emphasis on the role of society in fostering and providing the potential for leisure.

Policy Implications of a Psychological Conception of Leisure[20]

As indicated before, a residual (discretionary-time) conception of leisure carries policy implications of providing for the content of certain time periods and all that is related to and follows from such endeavors. A psychological conception, on the other hand, will focus policy considerations on the conditions necessary for generating a leisure experience. We are no longer limited to a part of the day (the unfortunate work-leisure dichotomy is fortunately nonexistent!), but are concerned with the total life of the individual, on any given day as well as throughout the life cycle. The scope of concern has been extended tremendously.

There are two broad categories of approach: (1) promoting conditions that are critical for the leisure experience, and (2) eliminating or at least ameliorating conditions that hinder the emergence of leisure. If we accept my model of leisure as a working hypothesis,[21] then the specific variables we shall have to deal with are perceived freedom and intrinsic motivation.

Translated into action, this means that we shall need to encourage those conditions which promote these variables and discourage those others which inhibit them.

The number of areas one could list for potential policy applications is enormous. I shall draw examples from a chapter of my forthcoming book, *To Leisure: An Introduction*, which deals with such areas within the context of the quality of life. First, I shall consider three very general topics, more for the record than with any expectations of implementation. These are utopian ideas, perhaps not so much in reference to Israel, but certainly in respect to the United States. I will then deal with policy suggestions that might have a chance of actual application. Lest the impression be given, however, that I tend to get carried away with grandiose, unrealistic ideas only, let me begin by illustrating through two concrete examples what I mean by increasing perceived freedom.

A training film on terminally ill patients showed an obviously severely weakened patient slowly getting out of bed, going to the window, and lifting the blinds. He then returned to his bed and stared out of the window. Somehow, these few seconds of the quite long film impressed me most. The patient was given the chance, in spite of his condition, to have an impact on the world, to change his environment, to be an "origin." He had the opportunity for choice, real alternatives, and he could act upon them. Are there other ways in which we could increase such opportunities for our institutionalized population? Small things, which would not involve major expenses but would perhaps be merely slight chances in routine?

The second example. A hospital served its patients breakfast in a room that had tables that would seat anywhere from two to perhaps twelve people. It served two kinds of toast (dark and white bread) and offered some other choices. Minor aspects, you might say, but perhaps just enough to turn a routine task into a leisure experience.

But back to the larger world: first, the "impossible dream." What would it take to create a leisure society? Freedom is as hard to achieve as it is to define. By restricting ourselves to perceived freedom, we have eased our task somewhat. Let us further introduce the distinction between *freedom from* and *freedom to*.

The first task of society is to provide for its citizens maximum freedom from the demands of everyday existence. This would minimally require a guaranteed health service and a guaranteed income. People would then be free from the fear of the economic consequences of sickness as well as from worry about subsistence needs. (I do not mean to imply that people ought to be free from all obligations or from their part in contributing to the common good.) Israel has probably more firsthand experience with social systems that have attempted to initiate these conditions than any other country in the world. Has providing these conditions necessarily led to an increased experience of leisure? We do not really have the answer, and I suggest that this is not a fair question or test of our assumptions.

At least a third step is necessary to realize a leisure society, and that is guaranteed education. However, this education needs to be one not only of knowledge (information required to accomplish the necessary jobs), but of values. We must first create a population that desires a leisure society! Does that sound like brainwashing? Yes, but does not every social system attempt to socialize its population along the lines of its values? Are we not here to mold leisure policies? Can we do this without having values?

Let us now return to a more mundane level and look at some specific areas for which a psychological conception of leisure carries policy implications.

Research

Social indicators, designed to measure the quality of life, are becoming important tools for policymakers. It is suggested that measures of perceived freedom and intrinsic motivation be developed and included in such indicators. We presently have no baseline data or information on differences in the perception of these variables among, for example, different occupations, home-related situations, free-time activities, institutional settings, or groups of people.[22] Do these factors contribute to experience? What is their role in the experience of the quality of life?

Leisure Education

While I have postulated the universality of the desire for leisure, I also recognize that people may be deterred from this goal for any number of reasons. "The public cannot know what it wants unless it is aware of, and has experienced, the alternatives which are available."[23] This statement reflects one of the possible reasons; others may be intrapersonal conflicts or personal-societal norm differences. Both leisure education and leisure counseling may be necessary to teach people "how to leisure."

Let me give a concrete example of leisure education as it relates to what I have called galloping consumption. This country is not so deeply infected yet by this phenomenon as is the United States; the more reason to prevent this from happening. The term refers to the obsession with possessions, the concern with "having." Space does not allow me to give the rationale why such an attitude is incompatible with leisure; but if we accept this premise, then leisure eduation means discouraging such an attitude and the resulting behavior.[24]

Another example refers to what I have called the right to know. It also touches on consumer behavior, but goes far beyond. Educate the public that it has a right to honest information about consumer goods and services and, yes, about politicians running for office. How does this relate to leisure? Perceived freedom requires a choice between meaningful alternatives, between toothpastes that really are different, and between the differences that really make a difference. Educate the public to demand its right to know, not only in the area of consumption of goods and services, but also for example, in the selection of news coverage on radio and television. Speaking for the conditions in the United States, it sometimes makes one really wonder how the public tolerates the kind of information that is presented as news, and particularly, what is left out.

The Political Arena

It is obvious that anyone concerned with improving the quality of life cannot avoid becoming involved in politics. This is true if you follow a residual conception of leisure,[25] and it is even more true if you adopt a psychological one. Every aspect of life is now evaluated within the framework of leisure, and leisure in fact becomes *the* criterion of the quality of life.[26]

If a country has a government that pursues an "enlightened" leisure policy, then the leisure activist ought to assist within that framework to provide optimal leisure conditions. If that is not the case, then an attempt ought to be made to arouse the consumer to action. There is no question that the creation of a leisure society, as envisioned, carries considerable political implications.

One final example. The very basis for a leisure society is freedom from toil brought about and made finally possible through our tremendous developments in science and technology. It is clear, however, that a technological breakthrough is not going to help if the benefits derived are reaped by a few individuals rather than by society as a whole. If this sounds revolutionary, it is. If it sounds like a dream, perhaps. But, let me end by quoting from my forthcoming book:

> The wish of having our country run by philosophers may be an idle dream, but the thought that it is run by bankers and businessmen is a nightmare. If we are serious in wanting to achieve a leisure society, we must confront the fact that the profit motive cannot be the guiding principle in such a society. . . The reader may feel that I am pushing too hard or that I am drawing the picture in extreme shades. But we are fighting for high stakes. We have heard it said many times: peace is a dangerous thing; it is obviously more difficult to achieve than war. It is even more difficult to maintain; and no nation has yet succeeded in maintaining it forever. Yet, we are reaching the point where we, the people of this planet, can no longer afford the folly of wars and where by necessity, we must settle for peace. In peace, however, lies the very condition for leisure, and with peace may finally come the Age of Leisure.[27]

NOTES

1. S. de Grazia, *Of Time, Work and Leisure* (New York: Doubleday, 1962), p. 414.

2. E. Katz and M. Gurevitch, *The Secularization of Leisure: Culture and Communication in Israel* (London: Faber & Faber, 1976).

3. P. 35.

4. P. 6.

5. J. Neulinger, *The Psychology of Leisure* (Springfield, Ill.: Thomas, 1974); idem, "The Need for the Implications of a Psychological Conception of Leisure," *Ontario Psychologist* 8, no. 2 (1976): 13–20; idem, *To Leisure: An Introduction* (Boston: Allyn & Bacon, 1981).

6. Neulinger, *Psychology of Leisure;* idem, "Psychological Conception of Leisure"; idem, *To Leisure.*

7. De Grazia, *Of Time, Work and Leisure*, p. 5.

8. Note that in the United States the predominant content of leisure (free time) tends to be seen as recreation rather than culture.

9. R. F. Green, *Work, Leisure, and the American Schools* (New York: Random House, 1968), p. 71.

10. Neulinger, *Psychology of Leisure;* idem, "Psychological Conception of Leisure"; idem, *To Leisure.*

11. I have not empirically explored the ranking of the desirability of mental states (e.g., anxiety, boredom, love, sadness, tranquillity), but I would place leisure at the top of such a list.

12. R. de Charms, *Personal Causation: The Internal Affective Determinants of Behavior* (New York: Academic Press, 1968).

13. R. W. White, "Motivation Reconsidered: The Concept of Competence," *Psychological Review* 66 (1959): 297–333; E. L. Deci, *Intrinsic Motivation* (New York: Plenum, 1975).

14. S. R. Maddi, "The Search for Meaning," *Nebraska Symposium on Motivation* 18 (1970): 137–86.

15. M. Csikszenthimalyi, *Beyond Boredom and Anxiety* (San Francisco: Jossey-Bass, 1975).

16. E. Fromm, *To Have or to Be?* (New York: Harper & Row, 1976).

17. E. Fromm, *Escape from Freedom* (New York: Holt, Rinehart & Winston, 1941).

18. S. Ferenczi, "Sunday Neurosis" (1918), in idem, *Further Contributions to the Theory and Technique of Psycho-analysis*, 2d ed. (New York: Basic Books, 1950).

19. C. Berg and J. Neulinger, "The Alcoholic's Perception of Leisure," *Journal of Studies on Alcohol* 37, no. 11 (1976): 1625–32.

20. See also Neulinger, "Psychological Conception of Leisure."

21. Ibid.

22. An instrument, "What Am I Doing? [WAID]: A Self-Exploration," has been developed for such a purpose, and data are now being collected from various populations.

23. Katz and Gurevitch, *Secularization of Leisure*, p. 109.

24. A good example of how one's conception of leisure leads to different conclusions is the fact that Katz and Gurevitch (ibid., p. 158) subsume leisure and consumerism under one set of values. That really hurts!

25. "There is no use evading the fact that the Government *is* actively involved in cultural policy" (ibid., p. 41).

26. See J. Neulinger, "Leisure: The Criterion of the Quality of Life; a Psychological Perspective" (Presented as the Harold K. Jack Lecture, Temple University, Philadelphia, 20 April 1978).

27. Neulinger, *To Leisure*. pp. 220–21.

Concluding Remarks

Max Kaplan

As everyone here, I have been to many international meetings on leisure: in Warsaw, Varna, Dubrovnik, Paris, Prague, Rotterdam, Montreal, Brussels, Uppsala, and Tampa. I observe without hesitation that this conference in Israel was among the very best in terms of the presence of theorists, practitioners, and policymakers on the highest level; the magnificent setting of Jerusalem and Ein Kerem, the historic valley below us; the level of papers and discussions by Israeli and visiting scholars; the historic time at which we met, with new hope for peace in the area and prospects of cultural interchange; government officials literally waiting for recommendations from the conference; and not least, the organizational ability and personal charm of Hillel Ruskin, Israel's chief missionary-messenger in this field to the rest of the world.

Yet no meeting of three days can be expected to consider or answer everything that confronts us in this field, even though—appropriately enough in Israel—a miracle has been achieved in producing so many pertinent and important recommendations! Permit me to note a few matters we might have considered more fully.

Given the presence of leisure theorists, animators, and government policymakers, there might have been more attention given to the interrelationship of these roles—a sort of policy on policy, or metapolicy, as it is called by Professor Yehezkel Dror of the Hebrew University, perhaps the world's leading scholar on the process of arriving at public goals and implementations. In some publications, I have considered the leisure theorist (because now I live in the woods of Alabama) as a little woodpecker on the trunk of a tree: our fanatic mission is to peck away, making little pointed noises. We look down, and on the ground are many busy ants, highly organized in their colonies of anthropologists, economists, information theorists, historians, psychologists, and (the queen over all, of course) the sociologists. And looking up, the oft-lonely woodpecker sees many birds floating in the air, migrating with winds, fashions, and seasons: the educators, social workers, recreation leaders, legislators—all those who apply the knowledge that comes out of the disciplines among the roots, integrated at the middle level by those of us who peck, peck, peck away. It is the right of the birds to avoid the trunk, going directly to any source of knowledge at hand, such as psychology, and their right—nay, their responsibility—to become enthusiastic over their goals; the recreation leader must defend and forward the enriching qualities of leisure. It is the right of root disciplines like psychology to maintain a neutrality, reporting the facts as they test and retest them. It is our right as leisure theorists on the tree trunk to draw upon the roots and the birds, to integrate theory and policy, to relate this tree to the whole forest of life and society. By studying trends, we see other forests being planted or destroyed, and we make our observations known to those below us and above us.

To leave this rural fantasy into an urbane philosophical mood, we might say that leisure, like other aspects of life, lends itself to discussion by those many disciplines which utilize the analytic tools available to them; those who value the assumptive tools, the policymakers, who protect the values of the society; and our role, as theorists, is to integrate the new and the old with creative instruments. But whatever our models, systems of analysis, or analogies, communications have to be pursued so that the respective roles and responsibilities can be clarified as the recommendations of this conference are considered after we leave. One would hope that Israel, with its relatively small size, could help set the direction of such communications. One of the tasks I have set for myself is to attempt the construction of a model for leisure policy, moving from the largest frame—the international—through cultural areas, nations, regions, communities, institutions, and ending with persons. National "case studies" will be crucial in that task, and this conference indicates that Israel is a microcosm of the highest importance for the world to study.

A second area of discussion for one from the outside is the relation of social tensions to leisure theory and policy. Hillel Ruskin's model touched on this, as did the paper by Professor Katz. Tensions, personal or collective, need not be destructive. As the analyst Viktor Frankl noted in a conference during the Munich Olympics, life without tensions can be empty; sports and arts create tensions in formal or stylized ways. The issue is not their presence, but the nature of their resolution. We read often in the literature about Israel that your education and politics are deeply involved with conflicting values; the oriental-occidental difference is only one of them. How can leisure patterns become more useful in a creative synthesis, with full respect to all backgrounds within your nation? What can other nations, such as my own, learn from you as we seek to preserve pluralistic values and practices and to minimize the uniformity wrought by, among other causes, our bland mass media?

Other issues could be listed. There is only one answer that I can suggest to Hillel, speaking for those of us from various parts of the world: that he invite us all back here for another productive conference. By then the Israelis will have applied many of our recommendations. With the experience as our laboratory, a new miracle can be set—yes, in three days—to pose and to solve all the issues that confront the theorist, the policymaker, and the diverse groups in our many cultures!

List of Seminar Participants

Participants from Abroad

LIVIN BOLLAERT, Ph.D., Free University of Brussels, Belgium
MAX KAPLAN, Ph.D., United States
RICHARD G. KRAUS, Ph.D., Temple University, Philadelphia, Pennsylvania, United States
JOSEPH LEVY, Ph.D., University of Waterloo, Ontario, Canada
GUSTAV MUGGLIN, European Leisure and Recreation Association, Zurich, Switzerland
JOHN NEULINGER, Ph.D., City College of the City University of New York, New York, United States
BERT RAES, Ph.D., Free University of Brussels, Belgium.
SAUL ROSS, Ph.D., University of Ottawa, Ontario, Canada
JEAN ROUSSELET, M.D., Centre d'Etudes de l'Emploi, Paris, France
F. W. SCHAPER, German Association of Leisure, Federal Republic of Germany
JAY S. SHIVERS, Ph.D., University of Connecticut, Storrs, Connecticut, United States
JAAP SWART, Recreation Association, The Hague, Netherlands

Participants from Israel

SHLOMO ACHITUV, Ministry of Education and Culture, Jerusalem
HANA ADONI, Ph.D., Hebrew University of Jerusalem
MARGALIT AKIVIA, Tel Aviv
AVNER AMIEL, Jerusalem Municipal Government
MOSHE ARI, Association of Community Centers, Safad
COLONEL DAVID BEN-ASHER, Israel Defense Forces
AMILIA AVIEL, Ph.D., Bar-Ilan University, Ramat Gan
HAIM DAGAN, Ministry of Education and Culture, Tel Aviv
ZVI DAGAN, International Cultural Center for Youth, Jerusalem

ZVI FEIN, Ph.D., American Joint Distribution Committee, Jerusalem

YA'ACOV GIL, Jerusalem, Municipal Government

MORDECHAI GRUNER, Jerusalem Municipal Government

ARIE HALEVI, Wingate Institute for Physical Education and Sports, Netanya

YARDENA HARPAZ, Ph.D., Corporation of Community Centers, Jerusalem

SHALOM HERMON, Ministry of Education and Culture, Jerusalem

MAUREEN HOLTZER, Mental Health Center, Haifa

HASINTO INBAR, Ministry of Education and Culture, Jerusalem

ELIHU KATZ, Ph.D., Hebrew University of Jerusalem

URI LIPZIN, Beersheba Physical Education Teachers College, Beersheba

DAVID MAKAROV, D.S.W., Hebrew University of Jerusalem

YARIV OREN, Ministry of Education and Culture, Jerusalem

DAVID REZNICK, Jerusalem

DAN RONEN, Ph.D., Ministry of Education and Culture, Jerusalem

HILLEL RUSKIN, Ph.D., Hebrew University of Jerusalem

BOAZ SHAMIR, Ph.D., Hebrew University of Jerusalem

MIRIAM SHMIDA, Ph.D., Bar-Ilan University, Ramat Gan

YOSI TALGAN, Jerusalem Municipal Government

GILAD WEINGARTEN, Ph.D., Wingate Institute for Physical Education and Sports, Netanya

HAIM ZIPPORI, Corporation of Community Centers, Jerusalem

Name Index

Subject Index

Propaganda, 90
Public education campaign, 18, 20, 80, 99

Quality of life, 15, 18, 67

Reading, 37–38, 53
Recreational experience, 104
Recreational needs, 111, 113, 122
Recreation context, 114
Recreationist, 107–8, 111, 120
Regression, 116
Required activity, 157
Residential environment, 120–21
Resources, 24, 77, 78
Routine, 105

Sabbath, 35, 37–38, 47, 49, 53
Scandinavian countries, 126
Scheduling approach, 162
Secularization of leisure, 172
Self-actualization, 104, 143
Self-directed activities, 111
Self-expression, 105, 118
Self-realization, 104
Sense of sacrifice, 166
Shorter workweek, 15, 36, 40, 47
Skiing facility, 127
Social integration, 122
Social interaction, 122
Social marketing, 90–91, 95, 97–99
Social-psychological needs, 54–55
Social security administration, 153
Social well-being, 169
Societal mores, 166
Society: and leisure, 157; of organizations, 165
Special Olympics, 127

Sports and fitness, 16, 68, 70, 84
Sports Participation Canada, 85–89, 94–96, 98–99
"Sunday Neurosis," 175

Therapy, recreation continuum, 128
Third World, 31
Tourism, 16, 55
Triggering mechanism: in Systematic Model of Leisure, 137

Unemployment, 147
UNESCO, 46, 59
Urban framework, 16, 69, 70, 116
Urban ghetto, 110
Urbanization, 116

Voluntary agencies, 169

"Weekend neurosis," 159
Western decadence, 167
Wild life conservation, 109
Work: and leisure, 24, 46, 60
Worker boredom, 161
Work ethic, 148
Working hypothesis, 175
Working model, 45, 46
Workshops, 109
Work time, 120
Work trends, 144
World Leisure and Recreation Association (WLRA), 27, 42, 59

Yom Kippur, 37

Zoological garden, 111